"Imagine if music history had eac[h] broken cable, exhausted magnetic [...] take centre stage. Through the pione[...] this book punches a series of holes [...] to drag you through the joys and curses of sonic [...] obsolete technologic patchworks and outcast techniques. For those who dwell in the uncertain fields of broken frequencies and hijacked transducers, this is it."

Artetetra Records

"Enrico's doting warmth for all things lo-fi will surely enchant you. Expect to find yourself perusing the dusty shelves of your local charity shop for a half working cassette deck the moment you close this book. Do you want to know why 'bad' is really good? Start reading!"

A.S., Grime Stone Records

"Whether it is marble or wood, color or sound, art is a fool's bet: our freedom can only be found by manipulating the sensible matter of our world. Enrico Monacelli's book shows that in order to save freedom, artists are capable of getting rid of their own art. *The Great Psychic Outdoors* is not only a history and theory of Low Fidelity. It is the most urgent aesthetic treatise of our century."

Emanuele Coccia, author of *Metamorphoses*

"Many will buy this book for the sonic adventures it promises, only to find themselves down unexpected rabbit holes of radical politics and philosophical inquiry. It is an experience to be cherished. We don't tend to write books about music like this anymore. But we should."

Matt Colquhoun, author of *Narcissus in Bloom*

"I'm so glad someone has finally written a book like this. It helped me realize all the reasons why I love lo-fi music — why it's been so important to me in my life, and why it deserves greater attention and recognition."

Constant Smiles

"A well written and informed intro into the world of lo-fi interweaving politics, philosophy and Enrico Monacelli's own interpretations of his favourite artists and the albums they crafted. A great overview for those new to the genre and a must read for anyone wanting to know more."

Thomas Crang, **gorgeous bully**

"Enrico Monacelli is the Kodwo Eshun of lo-fi. Blending urgent theory with carefully picked albums this magical essay takes us on a journey through the desert of acoustic vagueness. What does it mean to be an electronic loner in a crowded world? Encounter a gallery of one-off geniuses that produce now or never tracks, donated to the universe. There's a pleasure in wasting talent. *The Great Psychic Outdoors* is today's bible of outsider glam. Read about lo-fi as a sovereign act of slackerdom. Indulge in the dreamy stream of consciousness that turns madness into sound. Glide over clouds of undefined moods. Ride waves of foggy meanings, where music drifts off into noise, cut-ups, soundscapes, echoes, feedback and other imperfections — and listen how poetry derails."

Geert Lovink, author of *Sad by Design*

"When the world is too much, when everything is just too slick, too smooth, too processed — that is when lo-fi music, thanks to its very subtractions, can take us someplace else, someplace new. In this book, Enrico Monacelli guides us through the surprising varieties of lo-fi experience."

Steven Shaviro, author of *The Cinematic Body*

THE GREAT PSYCHIC
OUTDOORS

THE GREAT PSYCHIC OUTDOORS

Lo-Fi Music
and
Escaping Capitalism

Enrico Monacelli

Published by Repeater Books

An imprint of Watkins Media Ltd

Unit 11 Shepperton House

89-93 Shepperton Road

London

N1 3DF

United Kingdom

www.repeaterbooks.com

A Repeater Books paperback original 2023

1

Distributed in the United States by Random House, Inc., New York.

Copyright © Enrico Monacelli 2023

Enrico Monacelli asserts the moral right to be identified as the author of this work.

ISBN: 9781914420603

Ebook ISBN: 9781914420610

All rights reserved. No part of this publication may be reproduced, stored in a retrieval system, or transmitted, in any form or by any means, electronic, mechanical, photocopying, recording or otherwise, without the prior permission of the publishers.

This book is sold subject to the condition that it shall not, by way of trade or otherwise, be lent, re-sold, hired out or otherwise circulated without the publisher's prior consent in any form of binding or cover other than that in which it is published and without a similar condition including this condition being imposed on the subsequent purchaser.

Printed and bound in the UK by TJ Books

To M. N.
True love will find you in the end

For beauty is nothing but the beginning of terror which we are barely able to endure, and it amazes us so, because it serenely disdains to destroy us. Every angel is terrible.

R. M. Rilke

I was just thinking that the real world wasn't enough, that science isn't enough, that a true mistake is some kind of magic, or maybe God.

H. Korine

CONTENTS

Teenage interzone

On lo-fi and escape

> *We escape from the house*
> *As the day disappears from the sky*
> *Into night*
> *We became what we wanted to be*
> *Like a dream or a ghost*

Bright Eyes, "The Awful Sweetness of Escaping Sweat"

I have the weirdest memory of the first time I listened to Smog's "Teenage Spaceship". Extremely hazy and distinctly sharp. A real-life teen dream.

It was 2010 and I was seventeen. I plugged my headphones into my rickety laptop, a comically large piece of cheap plastic, full of wires and metal, that my parents bought for me. It was so cheap it would snap in half a few months afterwards. I chose the song randomly, based solely on the title, out of all the tracks on Smog's 1999 album *Knock Knock*. I had probably found the record on some random blog, one of many I would peruse at the time. A scant paragraph written by an overly excited someone somewhere in the world must have lured me in, but the details of the encounter faded somewhen along this last decade. If I think about it long enough, I can still recall the sinking feeling in my chest as Bill Callahan stumbled, like a morphine angel, on those few sparse, jagged lines crowning the heart of the song: "So large on the horizon/People thought my windows were stars/A teenage spaceship". If only I could make you feel such bliss!

The lyrics were grotesque, wired up with this unnameable, disquieting excitation. They painted a horrific, inhuman picture; a tiny Junji Ito-esque sketch. All sung from the first-person perspective, the track recounted the tale of a young boy turned inside-out by a machinic puberty. His body did not grow hair or pimples, but aluminium wings and thick glass windows. Adolescence made him a spaceship, an apocalyptic machine like Tetsuo, hovering over his hometown and outside the grasp of the adult world. The boy would only land at night, presumably, I thought, to avoid being captured by the boring life of the grown-ups. "I was beautiful with all my lights," concluded Callahan, aching at the memory of the wild flight — obviously and tragically snuffed out of existence, once and for all, by the drudgery of mandatory adulthood, but always haunting.

In an interview on the concept of adolescence, the philosopher and clinician Félix Guattari claimed that adolescence "constitutes a real microrevolution, involving multiple components, some of which threaten the world of adults. It is the entrance into a sort of extremely troubled interzone where all kinds of possibilities, conflicts and sometimes extremely difficult and even dramatic clashes suddenly appear", an outsideness, psychedelic and dizzying, unbound from any sort of "specific phase", natural cycle or physiological period, always pressing against the dreariness of so-called normal life. While singing "Teenage Spaceship", Bill Callahan was certainly living and dying by this savage interzone.

As surprising as it may sound, the first time I listened to the lyrics of "Teenage Spaceship", they did not strike me as particularly odd or off-putting. I could recognize the surreality of the story being told, of course, but it hit something quite quotidian inside of me. A relatable disorientation, so to speak. Wasn't my adolescence just as absurd, after all? I could easily recognize my joy and loneliness in the iron boy's wanderings. I snuck cosily in that excited outsideness and I could see myself, a few years down the line, melancholily pondering on my own unruly teenage ride. Once I would eventually wind up with my back against the wall, surrendering my revolutionary dreams to the demands of the adults, I could picture myself, guitar in hand, singing something like that.

And something else really caught me off guard: the song sounded skeletal and poor. Of course, I had already listened to the occasional badly recorded demo tape or scuzzy punk band, but there was something more to it. This track sounded *rough in an enchanting and premeditated way*. The guitar circled around those few chords, tense and unadorned, seemingly bouncing off small bedroom walls. It was sharp and metallic, right in front of everything else in the song, and it came off as beautifully mangled. The synths, right beneath the guitar, rung like a truly bizarre oxymoron: soaring, yet cheap and dusty. Callahan's voice sat on this pile of golden detritus and the drums rolled in, sounding like tiny tin cans fetched in some corner of a deserted wasteland. The most striking thing out of all of this was, surely, that it was clearly not a lucky coincidence emerged from fortuitous means or beauty born out of the bites of sheer necessity: it was a conscious style, some sort of recording wizardry fine-tuned by Callahan and his producer, Jim O'Rourke. The song didn't just end up like this. It was a work of *virtuosic ruination*, something purposely

3

made to explore the potentials of sounds in low fidelity. It was beautiful.

From that moment onwards, I started scavenging for more and I found myself somewhat obsessed with *lo-fi* — an amorphous umbrella term, short for "low fidelity", which names all music made, more or less intentionally, to sound poor, rough or proper bad. Or, in other words, anything but hi-fi. I became, overnight, a fan of this ambiguous genre comprised of a weird lot of artists: outcasts, visionaries and hacks experimenting with the possibilities of what a fucked-up cassette recorder, a cackling mic and primitive musicianship could actually do. Falling down the rabbit-hole was easy, with all the spontaneous and dispersed archiving our digital network culture has granted us, and I soon discovered that "Teenage Spaceship" was hardly as lo-fi as contemporary music could get.

Lo-fi quickly became synonymous with my very own teenage interzone. It was the soundtrack to my moments of teen bliss. The Noughties' somewhat lo-fi indie-pop — Clap Your Hands Say Yeah! above any other band — in the air in the skate parks we made ourselves in the remnant spaces our suburbia couldn't capitalize on. The Mountain Goats after my first dates. Guided By Voices as soon as I felt adolescence slip under my fingertips. Teen Suicide on the long commutes from my suburbia to Milano. Lo-fi has truly been the sound of those moments, so precious, when work and money and death were things I did not really understand — or when, at least, I could leave them lingering on the edges of my existence. Before modern life fully took hold of me, that is.

But despite its importance for me, no thorough theory on lo-fi music is to be found. I thought to myself, many times, that I would have liked to write about this thing I loved so much, not to explain away my love with some unitary theory, but to use it, somehow, to talk about me and my world, or even just to make heads-or-tails of what my loved one did to me and my world, and I always found myself incredibly alone. No one seemed to bother writing about it — or, at the very least, not as monomaniacally as I would have liked. I expected at least one book, but nothing came up. The only glaring exceptions were a handful of brave pioneers dedicating a few cultural studies articles to circumscribed features of the phenomenon, or talking about it in passing, but that was about it. Was I the only one who cared this much? Unlikely. Many would geek out about it. Was writing such a book an impossible task? Maybe.

Hito Steyerl came close. In 2009, she published one of the most insightful and biting defences of low fidelity I've ever read. It was titled *In the Defense of the Poor Image*, stating, plainly and from the very beginning, its aim: mounting a defence of a certain haunting poverty in our visual culture. According to Steyerl, this defence was necessary because the internet had been a vector of propagation of poor images on an unprecedented scale, leaving us stranded and disoriented. Our lives were suddenly flooded by strange creatures: "a rag or a rip; an AVI or a JPEG, a lumpen proletarian in the class society of appearances, ranked and valued according to its resolution". Visual low fidelity had become an extraordinary cultural force, reshaping our shared collective consciousness. A micro-insurrection happening silently all over the world:

> The poor image is an illicit fifth-generation bastard of an original image. Its genealogy is dubious. Its filenames are deliberately misspelled. It often defies patrimony, national culture, or indeed copyright. It is passed on as a lure, a decoy, an index, or as a reminder of

its former visual self. It mocks the promises of digital technology.

As much as I wholeheartedly agree with her characterization of the powers of aesthetic poverty, lo-fi music's absence in her analysis sticks out like a sore thumb. I don't blame her for focusing mostly on images, of course; in our aggressively visual culture, her defence of the poor image was not only called for, but necessary. Attacking the constant image-drone that underpins our lives with new critical tools was probably the best thing she could do, but still, why not take the obvious leap and look at what was up with poor sounds? What made lo-fi so utterly *unspeakable*? Why was giving an explanation to that haunting teenage revolt such a forbidden task?

My breakthrough came suddenly and unannounced, like a jump-scare or a conversion. I was not looking for it. My lo-fi book sat firmly beside the other hypotheticals. It came at the very end of that interview Félix Guattari gave on adolescence, in the form of a passing remark he threw out, then and there, probably to conclude the whole thing. It was about his teenage son. According to Guattari, his son was not into "politics" in the classical sense of the term. He paid no mind to The Party or The State or The Economy. But he was a political agent, nonetheless: he had a homemade free radio, a lo-fi project through and through. Says Guattari: "my son is into politics. Not so much through discourse, but with his soldering iron: he sets up 'free radios,' where technical discourse is hooked right into politics". Guattari's son was changing the world, not by any traditional, politically engaged means, but by going with teenage bravado straight to the wires, hijacking the airwaves, hacking the pop machine. In that moment, lo-fi's savage, teenage interzone started to make sense.

I soon discovered that what sounded like an off-handed comment to finally satiate an avid interviewer was far from being an inconsequential little thing for Guattari. His interest in free radio, this ancestral predecessor of lo-fi production, was a love affair deeply rooted in his personal and theoretical life. Free radios were an integral part of his redefinition of politics and political involvement — a post-political politics, if you will. He would often state that the appearance of a free radio "betrays, first of all, a collective sense of being 'fed up' with official media", a will to redefine our communal lives outside of State-and-Capital-sanctioned modes of existence. And he would often insist that producing something like a free radio (or a lo-fi record, we might add) was not just a "symbolic" protest against the status quo, but a direct act of escape from the quotidian. A jailbreak, so to speak, that he would define as a "molecular" movement, a drifting outside of normality's strictures and coercions through the irreverent use of each and every eccentricity, technical quirk and opening in the fabric of everyday life. An escape that could virtually produce new, freer ways of being one's self. Guattari described these molecular movements as follows:

> What characterizes the "molecular" is that the lines of escape combine with the objective lines of deterritorialization of the system to create an irrepressible aspiration for new areas of freedom. (One example of such an escape line is the free radio stations. Technological development, and in particular the miniaturization of transmitters and the fact that they can be put together by amateurs, "encounters" a collective aspiration for some new means of expression).

For Guattari, the most prominent practical example of these sorts of escape tactics was Radio Alice, a free radio that sprung up in Bologna in 1976, amidst the feverish peak of Italy's Years of Lead. Radio Alice appeared in Via del Pratello 41, a mercurial creature living in a ceiling somewhere along the narrow streets that crisscross Bologna's heart. People would come and go through the radio's DIY studio, a veritable continuation of an unruly street life. It was one radio among a true explosion of free radios in Italy at the time and it considered itself a *militant political intervention* with one mission: to steal RAI's (Radio Audizioni Italiane, the Italian national broadcasting company) state monopoly of radio frequencies. Take back the airwaves, break down and out of State control. The first song they played was Jefferson Airplane's "White Rabbit", a song perfectly fitting for a radio that found its main inspiration in Lewis Carroll's absurdist psychedelia. Everyone involved in the sonic militant intervention was, somehow, a deserter and an escapee, even its poor technical apparatus: the song was broadcasted from an old military transmitter, a Collins, that had been used to send out signals from tanks in the Second World War. The mere existence of this free radio, the reality of this escape, would give the conspirators a galvanizing, paradoxical certainty: "The revolution is just, possible and necessary: look comrades, the revolution is probable".

Free radio was part of a tapestry of political experiments that were trying out, both on a practical and theoretical level, a heretical version of Marxist critique (that Guattari was heavily involved in), updated to combat both the dreariness of the PCI, the official Communist Party, often accused with utmost scorn of being "Stalino-fascism", and a capitalist system mutating at breakneck speed. According to its "merciless prosecutor", this movement, often called Autonomia, was "a veritable mosaic made of different fragments, a gallery of overlapping images, of circles and collectives without any social organization", but whose impact was felt through myriad escape plans that would challenge the form of normal social life: "pranks, squats, collective reappropriations (pilfering), self-reductions (rent, electricity, etc.), pirate radios, sign tinkerin'". The autonomists did not care for seizing power nor opposing the State in a classical sense; they wanted to exit it altogether.

The most coherent conceptual picture to come out of this tumultuous patchwork is probably Paolo Virno's idea of a *social revolution as an exodus*. According to Virno, the novelty of these forms of struggle was the appearance of "proliferation of the *concrete* and the *different* within socialized labor", an outbreak that "requires a constellation of materialistic concepts which are totally detached from that universality characteristic of the 'general equivalent' and which are not used as the bases or synthesizing elements for the actual processes of liberation". This movement had unearthed the importance of doing things concretely, and doing them in a practically different way than the generally accepted way. "The 'technical-scientific intellect', 'off-the-books' labor, the feminist movement, young proletarians, etc. may be seen as parts — not reducible to any whole — of a composite praxis in which production and emancipation are intertwined." This insight lead Virno to theorize, inspired by Albert Hirschman's economic thought, a practice of exiting and escaping. Or, in other words, an exodus from Capital and the State through struggle and new, collective methods of deploying labour-power. "The political action of the Exodus consists, therefore, in an engaged withdrawal." This mode of engaged withdrawal would, of course, have nothing to do with the nationalistic exits we have witnessed in the recent past. It would be, on the contrary, a revolutionary and non-authoritarian form-of-life.

In simpler terms, according to Virno, *doing things concretely and otherwise* is a way to break the habitual patterns that our lives follow under capitalism. If workers in a factory, for example, share their knowledge of how things are made and start working in different ways (redistributing their roles and duties democratically, for example, or working less hours, or exiting the workplace altogether in order to use their labour-power otherwise), they can try to do those same things differently. By sharing the know-how and taking matters in their own hands, they put in question the whole structure of production: the chain of command, the division of labour, the way the worker's product is valued. This is precisely the reason why Virno says that this is some sort of exit or exodus: doing things differently critiques the structure of power and labour directly and it enables people to experiment with new ways of existing and inhabiting their world. It lets them exit the quotidian and enter new realms of existence.

This simple idea can, of course, be easily applied to everything we do under capitalism. And especially lo-fi music. After all, lo-fi is, at the heart of it, a way to record music yourself — poorly and roughly, for sure, but on your own terms. DIYing a track lets musicians question, directly and concretely, how music is made, under what conditions and even how that same music is valued and monetized. It shakes the habitual patterns of the music industry: the hi-fi studio-industrial complex.

Radio Alice died young. One night in March in 1977, a little over a year after its debut on air, the police raided the studio. Those were days of violent struggles in Bologna, but the police struck on an unusually quiet night. The radio kept rolling for the whole duration of the clear out. Someone shouts, "They're shooting! They're shooting!", as the police enter Alice's Wonderland. A sad rubble of tapes and destroyed equipment were the only things left behind. Radio Alice faded as Italy descended into one of its darkest, most terrifying periods: years of terror, paranoia and defeat. The cynical, dreamless Eighties would soon roll in, dispelling the hope of a revolution already won. Radio Alice fizzled out in the shadows of desecrated revolutionary dreams, leaving behind a trail of dazzling ideas and an undying sense of loss.

As I fell in this maelstrom of visions born out of psychedelia and struggle, lo-fi's teenage interzone started to fall into place: it, of course, bore no direct relation to these stories and concepts, but seen under the knife of this conceptual toolbox — escape, exodus, experimentation — it revealed its potential significance. Seeing Radio Alice as an early, hyper-politicized instance of lo-fi sonic practice led me to believe that even the least ideological forms of lo-fi music could be fruitfully analysed with the same lenses — as forms of tentative escape, sometimes catastrophic and other victorious, and exercises in doing artistic things concretely and differently. And on a very superficial level, it clicked perfectly; that haunting adolescence that lured me in certainly worked well as an immediate representation of an aesthetic, political and existential exodus, with its thrills and its downfalls. I did not have explanations nor certainties, but I had workable leads.

The following pages are, therefore, my experiment with lo-fi's teenage outsideness. I have constructed a "genealogy" of lo-fi music, a genealogy that will be neither a canon nor a complete history, and I put it under duress. We'll see how these concepts mutate when confronted with this cast of misfits and rockstars and weirdos, the lifeblood of the lo-fi movement. Will they bend? Will they break?

But before I begin, two methodological notes and a statement of intent:

Firstly, when I say that I will construct a genealogy, which is neither a history nor a canon, I'm following the rules that Foucault, after Nietzsche, laid out for all future genealogists. According to Foucault, a genealogy is a critical survey meant to highlight the breaks in human history. While history constructs a linear narrative, where the later things necessarily descend from the former, a genealogy instead highlights how each thing that happened constituted a rupture, the incursion of something new. If history is linear and conservative, genealogy is non-linear and disruptive, underlying difference and novelty, rather than progression and continuity. Or as Foucault himself would put it:

> Genealogy is gray, meticulous, and patiently documentary. It operates on a field of entangled and confused parchments, on documents that have scratched over and recopied many times [...] [Paul Rée, an historian of morality] ignored the fact that the world of speech and desires has known invasions, struggles, plundering, disguises, ploys.

I will not ignore these invasions. On the contrary, I will ditch any presupposition of continuity and present each artist as a forking pathway — irreducibly new and meaningfully disruptive.

And speaking of the artists, let me state why and how I chose them. I wouldn't say there's an obvious single criterion at play. Some were far too important to ignore; others are just personal favourites. And, as I said, this is not *The Complete History of Lo-Fi* or *Our Band Could Be Your Life*. Each artist does not continue or consolidate a supposed lo-fi tradition but constitutes a break in it. They all bring something new and irreducible to the table and I value them precisely because they are wholly irreducible to one another.

Nonetheless, they do have a couple of things in common: first, no matter how famous they were or became, they all preserved, more or less, a taste for the Outside. They're all nerds, freaks, queers incapable of assimilating into capitalist normality. They were or are incapable of completely complying, and I cherish them precisely because of their capacity to inhabit the outer fringes of our capitalist world. Secondly, by doing lo-fi music, they all directly put into question how things run under capitalism. With their mere act of doing things themselves, they concretely critique how music is produced. Their practice of sonic poverty in and of itself brackets the normality of the studio-industrial complex, with its undying hi-fi compulsions, and builds a savage interzone in the heart of contemporary music. And this act of defiant sabotage ought to be celebrated.

My lo-fi saboteurs will be seven in total, plus a small epilogue surveying the contemporary lo-fi landscape. Brian Wilson will be the first. He will be the embodiment of how the mere act of recording a lo-fi album can be a direct escape from the whole capitalist music industry. Then, it will be R. Stevie Moore's turn. The first proper lo-fi weirdo, R. Stevie Moore will show us how you can bring rockstardom to the masses through lo-fi. The third will be Daniel Johnston. He was an acid communist, just like Herbert Marcuse and Mark Fisher. My claim about him might seem preposterous at first, but, trust me, it's a trip but not a stretch. After that, I'll tackle Marine Girls and their sweet, weird, subversive femininity. Things will get a little darker with Ariel Pink and Perfume Genius: the first will be the emblem of escapes gone wrong and turned sour, and the latter will embody, with his heart-wrenching lo-fi ballads, all our contemporary sexual disquiet and the prospect of utopian care. At last, I'll deal with Mount Eerie and the dream of escaping this world altogether.

Lastly, allow me to spell out the thesis I'm working with: following Guattari's insight on free radios, I will work on the assumption that lo-fi, *in and of itself*, is a radical method of doing art. It is a practical subversion of sonic production under capitalism. And this sabotage of music-production is, in turn, a mode to create a weird outsideness within pop culture. A savage interzone, where rules and capitalist normality are upended and critiqued. I will always assume that lo-fi is a practical break from the present capitalist world. A sabotage of what there is. I will not ascribe a clear-cut agenda to lo-fi, though, since its weirdness has many guises and attains its peculiar characteristics mostly by how this sabotage is actually carried out. On the contrary, I will highlight how multiple agendas can be pursued through lo-fi. My own beliefs will, of course, be present in my analysis. I'd never try to pass my views as neutral or objective — I am clearly a Marxist with a partisan perspective on culture and the present. But I will, nonetheless, try to preserve a certain pluralism when it comes to the artists I'll engage with.

Results may vary. Only one thing is certain: in 1984, just a few days before Halloween, Thomas Pynchon defended the idea that there was a thin red line that connected political deserters and saboteurs to the history of the weird and the fantastic in contemporary culture; a cyphered lineage that ran from the luddites all the way to Frankenstein. The act of breaking machines, repurposing them and forcing them out of their quotidian routines was, according to Pynchon, the birthplace of the unspeakable and the miraculous, of all things that should not be there and that weird us out. "To insist on the miraculous is to deny to the machine at least some of its claims on us, to assert the limited wish that living things, earthly and otherwise, may on occasion become Bad and Big enough to take part in transcendent doings." Whatever happens after this book is through, that history will have a new chapter, one solely dedicated to lo-fi music, and our collective yearning for a fantastic, miraculous revolution will stand vindicated, once again.

I've been taken for lost and gone

Beach Boys and the birth of lo-fi

I'm writing a teenage symphony to God
Brian Wilson

Finding an origin is a perilous thing. It is rarely an innocent endeavour, a harmless pin-pointing of something's beginning. More often than not, it becomes a way to look for archetypes, hidden meanings, solid grounds. To nail something to a *fundamental, unshakeable truth* and create a story that falls linearly from that unmoveable nature, like a destiny or a curse. Discovering something's origin is, in other words, a way to control the thing itself, encasing its mutations, metamorphoses and changes in a straight line that runs from its incipit forwards to its very end, throughout its history, rationally and naturally. It is quite common to hear stories and biographies told as if they were entirely structured by some ancient Big Bang, a catastrophic or wonderful event happened in the murky waters of the narrated's infancy. A trauma or a virtuous coincidence. Most, if not all, of us live by the idea that Alan Moore once put in the mouth of Batman's most famous antagonist, the Joker: one bad day could make or break someone's or something's character completely, as if the microscopic shifts that occur in our day-to-day life were nothing in the face of this cryptic antecedent popped out of time's chaotic flow. And who isn't a sucker for a good origin story, after all? Is there anyone who could honestly say that they can resist the allure of a compelling narrative arc, starting from enthralling, definite premises and ending, consequentially, in tears or laughter?

Jean-Luc Nancy, a philosopher painfully aware of the daunting nature of origins, once wrote what could easily be considered a motto for anyone trying to come to terms with beginnings and willing to dispel the nefarious potential of origin stories: "The origin is a distancing". As it's always the case with philosophy's finest moments, the significance of this motto is at once very simple and perplexingly complex. If I had to give an abridged version of this powerful sentence, I'd probably say that what Nancy was trying to convey is that any origin whatsoever is never some hidden destiny or the appearance of an unshakable linear path, but a dynamic process that ripples down a plurality of pathways and existential back alleys that mutually diverge from one another. A beginning is always a discreet and plural affair, among many other "invasions, struggles, plundering, disguises, ploys" exploding all around. There's no cryptic truth to it, there's just something that distances itself from other things, kickstarting its proper existence. I've always found this idea exhilarating: being born and inheriting a history weren't stuffy curses anymore, but the abrupt untethering of something's existence from the bounds of the rest of the world. Off it goes, free to mutate at will!

A great practical example of this concept is a post on Reddit about the origin of lo-fi music. It was posted on September 29th 2012 by a now-deleted and therefore anonymous user.

I first read it as I was looking for a solid incipit for the lo-fi movement in general and this book in particular. It stood out to me because it was a post that, incidentally, encapsulated my very own idea of where lo-fi came from, my most natural guess about its inception. It also showed the sheer impossibility of claiming that lo-fi — or anything else, for that matter — has a precise beginning, easy to pin-point in pop culture's sprawling history. In a mad fit of confirmation bias, I stumbled on it because the anonymous poster and I shared the same intuition, a sort of germinal theory on lo-fi's origin I'd been incubating for a while: according to the both of us, lo-fi came, in some profound sense, from the Beach Boys and, more specifically, from Brian Wilson's fraught relationship with capitalism, beauty and pain.

The title of the post read: "The Beach Boys inadvertently established lo-fi as a musical aesthetic in the late Sixties, shaping indie records of the Nineties. Discuss." The user aided the discussion by further elaborating:

> Here's the low-down. It's '67, Brian Wilson has wasted masses of Capitol's money on the aborted *SmiLE* sessions and promptly suffers a mental breakdown, broke, studioless, and now without their principal songwriter, the Beach Boys still have contractual obligation to release [an]d album this year. They hunker down in Brian's living room and knock off an album in pretty much an afternoon (or so it sounds on the record), the result, *Smiley Smile* pretty much took the band out the arms race of musical progression they helped start with *Pet Sounds* and is still divisive (read, HATED) to this day. When

you listen to the record you can almost hear the cannabis smoke, as if it seeped into the magnetic tape in recording the album. This is lo-fi, by a mainstream act, in '67. It's no secret that the Beach Boys have been massively influential in indie music (just look at Fleet Foxes' debut), did they invent lo-fi as a genre as well?

Despite being just a crude, skeletal sketch, anyone could see that there's a great origin story here, one that looks rife with ideas and illuminations not only about lo-fi as music genre, but about lo-fi as a conceptual and aesthetic object in the contemporary music scene and the capitalist cultural industry as a whole. A story I, for a lack of better words, *vibed with* on an almost instinctive level — a good vibration, if you will. It foreshadowed Brian Wilson's lo-fi grandeur, his looming presence on all subsequent evolutions of this genre as a sort of archetypal incarnation of lo-fi's revolutionary potential, filled from the very beginning with Wilson's fiery, almost ecstatic discontent for the system he was so embroiled in. A promising lead for a genealogy of this weird creature. A good entry point to probe its political implications and surely a great way to narrativize where and when this strange thing came from.

But a beginning is always a plural affair and another user replied: "I'm not sure... *The Velvet Underground*, Paul McCartney's first two solo albums, *The Basement Tapes*, Neil Young's Ditch Trilogy, Skip Spence's *Oar*, Garage Rock as a whole — I think it's too reductive to trace lo-fi back to just one album's influence". "Springsteen's *Nebraska*, too," soon followed. Evidently, all these suggestions were, more or less, correct. From Paul McCartney writing quaint little melodies, perennially high on hashish and secluded outside of civilization's reach somewhere in Scotland, like the Unabomber in Montana or Ludwig Wittgenstein in Norway, to Bruce Spingsteen's gaunt, down-trodden Americana recorded on a cheap Teac Portastudio, each and every one of these suggestions was just as valid a beginning as any other. One could even divert their gaze further back and argue that modern rock music itself is rooted in lo-fi: the recordings of Alan Lomax, an ethnomusicologist whose archives strived to preserve popular and folkloric sound heritages, from the "American patchwork" of Black and dissident sonic cultures all the way to Italian magical chants and incantations, were, more or less directly and explicitly, a fundamental inspiration for all the rock music that followed. Those recordings, captured from the 1940s onwards, were in and of themselves quite raw and poor and, in a sense, lo-fi, albeit mostly due to technical contingencies rather than a deliberate aesthetic choice. The candidates for the spot of first proper lo-fi record were many, various discreet breakthroughs mutually diverging and creating their own personal story of how lo-fi came to be. Promising beginnings were popping up from every corner of the aboveground music scene and God only knows how many more contenders there could be if we took into account all of the glorious home-recorders of the world, partially or completely forgotten, privately spellbound by the wonders of the beautiful bad music they did themselves in their secret chambers dispersed around the world…

Frustrating as it clearly was, this observation forced me buckle under the evidence and admit the obvious: could it really be otherwise? Lo-fi has always been, since its very inception, a carnival parade traversed by many genres and a heterogenous barrage of artists and visionaries and freaks. Did I really expect one, clean-cut debut? A unifying backstory to tie all loose ends up in a singular, original knot? Nonsense! As far as I can see, the original, anonymous poster did not reply either.

This little shipwreck of mine had, nonetheless, instructive upshots. I still believed that the Beach Boys had a special connection with lo-fi's beginning, as if they were the veritable first step of some sort of cultural alchemical process that brought lo-fi as we know it into being, but I had to confront the questions and insights raised by all other possible candidates and their respective versions of the story. First and foremost, I had to face the fact that *objective* claims about the origin of lo-fi would have been dubious, or, at the very least, somewhat of a stretch. There was no one, hidden meaning there or some manifest destiny I had to uncover — the story was far more complex and intricate than that. Plainly demonstrating its profanatory nature from the get-go and proving Nancy's insight to be fundamentally correct, lo-fi defied the possibility of a capital-H History and the unifying pretensions of any capital-C Critics. Every origin story of lo-fi was always, from the very beginning, the expression of a partisan position, among many others, led by everything but the possibility of constructing a linear unfolding in the evolution of the genre and competing with conflicting and just as vital lineages. The ranks of the superstars that, by virtue or sheer necessity, decided to experiment with poor sounds was far too numerous and, behind them, loomed legions of DIY amateurs silently paving the way for things to come. Any account of how it began had to either be unreasonably long or decide to take sides, be somewhat personal and bound to a certain idea of what lo-fi is and does. It had to expound a specific vision not only of the music itself, but of its wider social aims and contexts and the artistic lineage it produced. Sure, Brian Wilson had experimented with the potentials of bad recordings at the end of the Sixties, beating most of the others to it from a chronological, objective point of view — with some evident, glaring exceptions. But still, the Beach Boys' importance for us and their primacy among the rest had to stem from a more insightful *why*, something that informed on a deeper level what lo-fi's revolutionary potential actually is. Something more than "they did it first". Vibing with something was not enough, obviously; I had to reach deeper and deeper and discover what made that specific origin story tick.

Secondly, and because of these first considerations, my own private Reddit Waterloo made clear another salient trait that any origin story required: a reason for crossing the threshold, for leaving hi-fi behind. Since there are so many possible beginnings every artist naturally embodied a different style of cheap recording. Was it by necessity? Did they choose it deliberately? Was it a fuck-you to the culture industry or a placid example of bedroom experimentalism? Each possible candidate had a specific reason, applicable almost exclusively to them and themselves only, and this reason had far-reaching consequences on the particular shade of lo-fi they brought into this world. It wasn't a mere dichotomy between hi-fi and lo-fi, but a spectrum of possible reasons to approach this craftmanship, reasons that had to do with the totality of the cultural ecosystem said artist was embedded in and that consequently resonated throughout the whole of their subsequent endeavour through its tone, mannerisms and posterity. The singular biographies and the million idiosyncrasies that forced this or that hand, that drove Paul McCartney or Lou Reed or Neil Young or Bruce Springsteen out of the studio-industrial complex and back to their living room or kitchen sink or secluded farm or communal space or wherever else, was not some meaningless contingency or negligible event. They created a special way of doing what they did, they forged the conceptual takeaway we could get from them. And, of course, precisely for this spectrum of incomparable reasons for dropping out and doing things poorly, woven into the artists' lives in the broadest possible sense, the conceptual baggage one could extract from one would not fit another, or, at the very least, would amount to a gross simplification. A destructive umbrella-termification that would annihilate the peculiar path that one artist had carved out for themselves and those that followed them, among the multitude of feasible beginnings and likely outcomes of the movement. In brief, I had to ask myself *why* I chose Brian Wilson at least twice as hard, and very specifically!

So, why Brian Wilson? What's so special about the Beach Boys?

Plainly speaking, Brian Wilson and the band that for a long time was something of a direct extension of his own peculiar genius, the Beach Boys, was the musician that more than any other embodied the idea of *lo-fi as escape*. An aesthetic practice with deep existential and political consequences — ambiguous, glorious, contradictory, unsettling, sometimes disastrous, sometimes promisingly weirding — meant to break out of the strictures and the drudgeries of contemporary capitalism. A way of making wonderous tunes fleeing from the chokehold of this world, forged in tragedy and beauty, fate and blind accidents. An acid lo-fi (lo-fidelia?) to turn on, tune in and drop out to — with every contradiction this entails. Not even Paul McCartney — whom Wilson himself regarded as his only kindred spirit — could come close to the weirdness Wilson stumbled upon with his explorations into lo-fi territories. In fact, while McCartney was, like Wilson and contrary to popular belief, an experimentalist at heart, in love with Stockhausen and neat studio oddities, who quite literally fled society to compose his own ground-breaking lo-fi records — *McCartney* in 1970, *Ram* in 1971 and *McCartney II* in 1980 — he was, at the same time and, this time, contrary to Wilson, bogged down by a certain underlining domesticity. His lo-fi experiments felt like little embryos floating in their peaceful amniotic sack, watched over by Paul and Linda McCartney's loving grace, in their idyllic embrace. Such a mythological quietude might be moving, but it couldn't hold a candle to Brian Wilson's psychedelic journeys at the edges of ecstasy and exhaustion, which, precisely for their strangeness, feel to me like the only natural starting point for a radical reading of the lo-fi phenomenon.

But too much, too soon! Let's roll back the tape and start from the beginning. A quite paradoxical one at that, since this story has to take its first steps from one of the most extraordinarily hi-fi records ever made: *Pet Sounds*. This album's hagiography has rightly become an integral part of rock 'n' roll history. Few albums have been praised and commented on as much as the Beach Boys' eleventh album. After all, it single-handedly took the Beach Boys out of their infantile sunshine shell, all surfing and sand-drenched fun, straight into the ethereal realm of an almost unheard-of form of baroque, harrowing pop music. A watershed moment in music history and our collective consciousness.

Pet Sounds was born out of a strange existential experiment: in 1964, Brian Wilson decided to leave the stage lights to the rest of the band, mostly composed of his brothers, to focus solely on music production. He was deeply fascinated by Phil Spector's radical approach to recording sounds, which upended the function of the studio and turned it into an instrument in and of itself. He decided that, from that moment onward, he would be wedded to the machine just like Spector. "I was unable," said Wilson, "to really think as a producer up until the time where I got familiar with Phil Spector's work. Then I started to see the point of making records. You're in the business to create a record, so you design the experience to be a record rather than just a song." Another contributing factor to his studio seclusion was surely a rampant competition he felt mounting with the Beatles, a band that was, according to Wilson, upping the ante of music-production to unbelievable standards:

> We recognized that the Beatles had cut *Rubber Soul*, and I really wasn't quite ready for its unity — it felt like it all belonged together. *Rubber Soul* was like a folk album by the Beatles that somehow went together like no album ever made before, and I was very impressed. I had to go in there [the studio] and experiment with sounds. I really felt challenged to do it — and I followed through with it.

The competition with the Beatles was, according to Wilson, a *never-ending spiral*, a quickly escalating musical arms race.

Wilson would hire the best session musicians he could find and toil endlessly on the inner workings of sounds, melodies and structures. He would explore all nooks and crannies looking for *something more*, something that would top anything that was ever recorded ever, devoting his artistic life to the craft of recording records rather than playing songs in front of other people — retreating to the relatively colder lair where sounds are artificially born, fleeing the ritualistic heat of the concert. In a sense, it could be easily claimed that he became solely interested with the *unconscious* of contemporary music: the studio, the material means of sonic recording, things ever obscured by rock's obsession with the grand, singular human presence of the star. From that point forward, this became a distinctive mark of Wilson's most accomplished output: an obsessive attention to the machinic, hidden reverse of pop, working like a mole on the cogs of the machines that spit out popular music rather than on its personalities and its manifest features. He became a psychoanalyst — perhaps a sonicanalyst — of contemporary music-making, and all of the Beach Boys' subsequent records turned into an overt study of what makes us tick, of the thing that pulls pop's stings and makes us sob and laugh and dance. A peculiar trait for someone who would end up becoming one of lo-fi's putative forerunners. *Pet Sounds* was the apex of this cyborgian union with the studio.

Wilson's fleeing the stage was not a purely artistic, disincarnate choice, though. In April of 1965, he had his first experience with acid, a substance that would prove both a breakthrough and a rupture for him. Talking about his first trips, he would happily confess: "I took LSD — a full dose of LSD — and later, another time, I took a smaller dose. And I learned a lot of things — like patience, understanding. I can't teach you or tell you what I learned from taking it, but I consider it a very religious experience". Acid clearly put him in contact with something outside the quotidian. A form of enjoyment unrestricted by the narrow confines of normality. But his trips exasperated his mental health as well. Acid alone could not abolish or relieve the pressure of a culture industry hellbent on forcing him to dish out hits at ever-accelerating pace and, in such conditions, it became poisonous for Wilson's mind. It turned out to be the beginning of the most astounding segment of his career and of a tragic downward spiral.

Schizoaffective symptoms manifested themselves, creeping up on him as auditory cracks in his consciousness, and he was forced to live with voices who would continually berate him. As he would later recall:

> Well, for the past 40 years I've had auditory hallucinations in my head, all day every day, and I can't get them out. Every few minutes the voices say something derogatory to me, which discourages me a little bit, but I have to be strong enough to say to them, "Hey, would you quit stalking me? F*** off! Don't talk to me — leave me alone!" I have to say these types of things all day long. It's like a fight.

One can only imagine how hellish the experience of the stage, with its dark pit of fans, and stardom's grind would become in such a state. "When I was on stage I could hear voices telling me negative things about myself. Even today, when I sing I have to force myself not listen to them. But when the concert is over, the voices come back." His depression, too, would worsen: "My depression goes pretty low, pretty deep. I get depressed to the point where I can't do anything — I can't even write songs, which is my passion".

Psychedelia was, for Brian Wilson, the experience of a profound cracking up of the self, both revolutionary and infernal, exposing both the misery of his and the world's material condition and the unexpected possibility for something else other than what we've got that lies dormant — somewhere, somewhen. Or as Deleuze once put it in flowerier terms: "A strafing of the surface in order to transmute the stabbing of bodies, oh psychedelia". An experience clearly pregnant with terrible truths about the world and Wilson himself, in much simpler terms. "It shattered my mind and I came back, thank God, in I don't know how many pieces." *Pet Sounds* was a way of exploring this shattering by other means, and outside the venomous constrictions that made psychedelia so noxious for Brian Wilson. Or, as Deleuze put it, a way to

> not give up the hope that the effects of drugs and alcohol (their "revelations") will be able to be relived and recovered for their own sake at the surface of the world, independently of the use of those substances, provided that the techniques of social alienation which determine this use are reversed into revolutionary means of exploration.

Given all these premises, it has become quite a cliché to consider *Pet Sounds* the product of "Brian's emotional fragility". The enchanting sound of someone about to blow up into a million pieces, locked up in the studio among machines and tapes gangling all around. And while this is somewhat of an inconvertible truth, to some extent I always thought it was a scandalously simplistic idea. It downplays the scope of *Pet Sounds*' discontent, a feeling that innervates the entirety of the record, reducing it to Wilson's individual trials and tribulations. Of course, someone's pain is always, in a sense, an island standing on its own, and I would never want to explain away the pain Wilson expressed so vividly with some wider narrative or overarching concept. There's always a gap in suffering: I can never reach out and directly touch your toothache or heartbreak or anything else. When talking about pain of any kind, one should never really explain but try to give a home to the sufferer to freely express their condition and what they believe is going on around them. But by the same token, one should never treat pain as something existing in a vacuum, punctual by itself, context-free. Every suffering is a suffering within certain conditions: existential, social, even cosmic if we're feeling adventurous. Human anguish is always something that has to do with humanity overall, in a given moment in time, and Brian Wilson's anguish is truly no different. Analysing an album so deeply tied to mental illness and pain, a record Wilson considered a veritable "sketchbook of his life", as an expression of private, emotional fragility, is mutilating: it deprives it of a great chunk of its meaning by excising the wider world it was made in. It tames its words and sound. Pain, like origins, is always an event that must be spoken of in plural, bound as it is to our fleeting existence, and it speaks to human existence in its entirety.

And Brian Wilson's expression of his suffering (and joy, of course) on *Pet Sounds* surely had a message for humanity as a whole: a will to escape and make something that would break out of the boredom and misery and relentlessness of the capitalist life, aided by the studio machinery to its highest potentials. To make a record that would just end this tiresome world and build a way out through the highest form of hi-fi production available at the time, that was the mission. Almost an apocalypse in pop.

Nowhere is this more apparent, in my opinion, than in the opener, "Wouldn't It Be Nice". A grand love song, sleek and enormous, full of teenage yearning. Two young lovers fused into one, wishing that every kiss was never-ending. The expression of someone hoping for something better, a purer passion and a happy ever-after. These interpretations, which are the most superficial and natural reading, don't exhaust the depth of the track, somehow relegating it to the most private strata of desire and to being a simple little love song. Just underneath this banal teenage longing, something else shines through: a deep frustration with a world full of enclosures, boundaries and scarce goods on all fronts, and an urge to transgress all of this. "It expresses the frustration of youth, what you can't have, what you really want and you have to wait for it", admitted Brian Wilson quite candidly. It is surely a feeling that is inherent to teen lust, but it finds in this song a bigger meaning untethered tò the physiological necessities of a specific age, elicited by the material constrictions of this world of ours. It is haunted, in other words, by the fear that even if youth might end eventually, these constraints won't be lifted:

> *Maybe if we think and wish and hope and pray*
> *It might come true.*

Brian Wilson was, after all, in his twenties and already married — shouldn't it be starting to get nice by then? The track expresses the same pent-up frustration Herbert Marcuse voiced just a short ten years prior when he wrote: "People dwell in apartment concentrations — and have private automobiles with which they can no longer escape into a different world. They have huge refrigerators stuffed with frozen foods. They have dozens of newspapers and magazines which espouse the same ideals. They have innumerable choices, innumerable gadgets which are all of the same sort and keep them occupied and divert their attention from the real issue — which is the awareness that they could both work less and determine their own needs and satisfactions."

You know it seems the more we talk about it
It only makes it worse to live without it.

Underneath the veneer of a sweet love song pulsed the teenage longing for "what capital must always obstruct: the collective capacity to produce, care and enjoy", as Mark Fisher once put it.

Right from the beginning, the need to escape and find somewhere better to live seems to be the crowning idea of Wilson's ear-candies. There's this lingering suspicion that this world, as it stands today, is quite *obscene*, not a nice place to be at all. Stuck in the churning mills of the culture industry and the capitalist world, Wilson seemed to long to pull a Houdini out of it all. His pain and desires were not coming exclusively from within his psyche, but also from the material conditions of his time, which were really much too cluttered and demanding and unsatisfying and soul-crushing. "Obscenity is not confined to sexuality, because today there is a pornography of information and communication, a pornography of circuits and networks, of functions and objects in their legibility, availability, regulation, forced signification, capacity to perform, connection, polyvalence, their free expression…" wrote Baudrillard, and it is hard not to think that Brian Wilson would have somewhat agreed.

Then "Sloop John B" kicks in and something breaks. As the first half of the album ends, the mask drops and the uneasiness with the capitalist world and the emaciated libidinal world it entails breaks loose. "Sloop John B", from the get-go, makes the disgust for the present palpable. It lets the yearning for something else out. Originally a Bahamian maritime folk tune, Brian Wilson discovered the song via the Kingston Trio, who recorded the track under the ominous title of "The Wreck of the John B". Clearly, this time around, it isn't a love song at all: it tells the story of a mariner stranded somewhere in the Atlantic. The lonesome fellow roams around Nassau high, drunk and beat, with a crew of incompetents and sea-fiends. He sobs all throughout the song:

> *I feel so broke up*
> *I wanna go home.*

The metaphor is plain to see. Brian Wilson is stuck in the studio, cabin-fevered and surrounded by tapes and odd instruments producing a million sounds, forced to keep the Beach Boys machine rolling to churn out more and more money for his label and the culture industry at large. He feels exhausted and done, he'd just like to go away and be happy. Find a home and be able to properly enjoy himself, the people he loves and his art. No wonder he felt like he was living in a sinking ship! He wanted to dissolve the bonds that kept him tied to a record label, the showbiz and the world economy all together. There's almost a folk horror, *Wicker Man*-esque element to the song: this wilderness (the open sea, the sinking ship, the raging crew) that reflects the neurosis of the moderns, the ones living under capitalism or, in other words, us. The obscenity Wilson feels around him is suffocating and the sweet bop serves only to convey all Wilson's teeth-grinding and fist-clenching. It's obviously a track sung by someone who thinks that his situation is insulting and depressing — who would like to let the listener touch his desire for a new world, his disgust for the one we've got. A blackened psychedelia permeates the song:

Why don't they let me go home?
This is the worst trip I've ever been on.

The sound of a world so small and cramped-up it has become unliveable. Of wanting better trips and a good life.

From this moment onward starts a drawn-out fade to black, one of the most moving in the history of pop music. The central theme, wanting to escape from this world while being stuck in it, becomes almost unbearably pressing: what does it mean to desire a post-capitalist world or life for us? Would this pain go away? Can we even begin to fathom such a new world? These questions are so overt that, along the way, we even find a song openly and unambiguously about not fitting into the hellish twisting-and-turning of capitalist America. We get so dangerously close to naming the thing we'd like to escape from: our current economic system. Almost an unabashedly anti-capitalist song, in other words. It is sung from the perspective of someone who keeps *looking for a place to fit*. He's good for nothing, albeit being told that he's smart. There's nothing wrong with him, really, but the world he lives in just won't let him find the things he needs. His emotional life is drained out by the vicissitudes of this empty quotidian existence. Revolutions, or, at the very least, some kind of comradery or something that would help him feel less alone in this rut, are nowhere to be found:

Every time I get the inspiration
To go change things around
No one wants to help me look for places
Where new things might be found.

There's no solidarity for him to keep his head above the water, no movement or community or organization to grant him the hope for a realistic way out, or even the fleeting shadow of some amelioration or solace. Is it even possible to dream something else? He blatantly suffers from a malaise Mark Fisher diagnosed in his most famous book, *Capitalist Realism* — the incapacity to even begin to fathom something other than the capitalist emotional and physical wasteland we have all inherited, foreclosing any social and communal action against the current state of things. "Reflexive impotence amounts to an unstated worldview […] and it has its correlate in widespread pathologies," and it's quite evident that capitalism made Wilson sick. The chorus goes: *Sometimes I feel very sad.* The song is called "I Just Wasn't Made for These Times" — even the title is a gut-punch.

Pet Sounds then crawls to its natural conclusion. After this sweet tour-de-force, the closing track, "Caroline No", feels like an apical moment — the feverish peak when all this tension is finally released. Tragically, I must add, since it turns out to be a darkened recapitulation of the opener, "Wouldn't It Be Nice"; a sad recurrence of its neurotic core. The song is, once again, an exercise in utmost ambiguity, exhausting what the album has been thus far: a sweet ballad about a bitter love slowly gnawed at by time and banality, consumed by sheer inertia. Two contrasting figures are meshed together contradictorily: Caroline, Wilson's high-school darling, the epitome of an enjoyment so full it breaks the bounds of reality; and Wilson's actual wife, with all the inevitable petty details that dot every relationship, presented here as the archetype of how things really are in their pallid, quotidian sadness. Even the title itself is somewhat like Janus: two-faced. This irreconcilable split is there even in the words that christen it. Read together out loud, they sound both like "Caroline No", a lament of profound discontent and refusal aimed at how things are, and "Carol, I Know", airing out all the resignation of someone having to live in a world that does not feel like home. Nothing is resolved and we're left in the midst of this impossibility to actually live according to our needs and desires, out of here. As the song dies out, I can't help but think that *Pet Sounds* sounds like the best prelude ever recorded. A long, majestic overture to something else, something that would actually accomplish the escape that haunts it. The beginning of a *vanishing act* that could only begin to be carried out through one of the many births of lo-fi music.

And given how things played out after the release of *Pet Sounds*, I'd say that mine is more than a feeling, but a faithful rendition of how Wilson himself felt about the record and the events that soon followed. Once he was done with it, he quickly began working on a record that would be far grander, a project that would top the enormity of the previous one. Despite the relatively mediocre sales, the record label wanted more, parading Brian Wilson as a new genius of the most absolute form of hi-fi pop music. There was also a new crop of artists was bursting onto the scene — Jimi Hendrix, the Doors, Jefferson Airplane — threatening to make even the most adventurous Beach Boys' psychedelic escapades seem tame and *passé*.

Pet Sounds was meant to be a transition or a first act, rather than a full stop soon to be supplanted by the ever-accelerating capitalist culture and its adversarial countercultures. This next project, a collaboration with songwriter Van Dyke Parks, was going to be called *SMiLE*, and it was finally going to be that reverie outside of this world that *Pet Sounds* had merely introduced. No more duplicities and frustrated desires. No boredom or misery would survive this next release: if escape was *Pet Sounds'* great mirage, its fading frontier and aching unconscious, in *SMiLE* it was bound to be a tangible reality. The real thing. Life and music conjoined in something bigger than everything else we've ever got. "In a scale of 1 to 10, I'd give *Pet Sounds* a 4 and *SMiLE* a 10", that's how Wilson saw it. "More exploring, more adventure". *A teenage symphony to God* — that's what he wanted it to be.

The recording process was harrowing. Wilson had taken up a reckless acid-and-cocaine toxicological diet, making the already complicated task of recording such a byzantine thing outright excruciating. "We [Brian Wilson and Van Dyke Parks] were so slowed on drugs we could only write 20 seconds at a time," he would later claim. On top of his chemical experimentations, Wilson was completely and, arguably, more fundamentally absorbed by an unshakeable creative mania, wholly possessed by something that was getting more and more out of his control. His study of pop's sonic unconscious had, from *Pet Sounds* onwards, produced unexpected results, leading him to places he probably had never imagined before.

Just like Guattari predicted in his analysis of free radios, messing directly with the machine itself, with the technical aspect of recording and making sounds, hooked Wilson up to some weird things: a barrage of political, existential and aesthetic questions he probably ignored before retreating to the studio and doing-it-himself. Questions that surely unsettled him, shaking him up and down to the very core of his identity as a musician within the music industry. He became convinced that he was creating the soundtrack to some sort of strange witchcraft, of his own studio sabbath. His recording seclusion had brought him into contact with unorthodox sounds and radical experimental methods, leading him to wanting to write a hall-of-mirrors-like rock opera where all conventions and norms, both social and artistic, were to be suspended and upended. Then an ominous fire broke out in the building across the street one day in early December. Wilson took it as a bad omen. Surprisingly, it actually was.

The record was never finished. After a while, for many reasons and vicissitudes, all quite controversial and unclear — which go from internal disagreements to Carl Wilson deserting the army draft and being jailed, as well as the release of *Sgt. Pepper's Lonely Heart Club Band*, an impossible record to beat to Wilson's ears — the project was declared defunct. In 2004, Brian Wilson published a re-vamped version of the album, *Brian Wilson Presents SMiLE*, and in 2010 the band released the remnant studio sessions, recreating a sense of what *SMiLE* once potentially was. But none of them were *it*, the forever-lost finished product. A handful of completed songs from that period were released over the years, most notably the perfect and hyper-famous "Good Vibrations" and the disquietingly gothic "Surf's Up", a Poe-inspired description of the dominoing ruins of a world we must leave behind, with its nauseating *blind class aristocracy* and all, giving a taste of how the impossible feat could have sounded, but the promised escape sank in the realm of the could-have-beens, eternally becoming a lost future that never was.

But the capitalist culture industry still wanted its due offering. Being the vampire it is, it couldn't take an "I can't" for an answer — it still had to suck the lifeforce and living labour out of something to produce some sort of value and gain for itself, after all. The Beach Boys tried to terminate their contract early, but they had the obligation of releasing another album pending on their heads. They had to come up with something.

Brian Wilson decided to opt for an unexpected Plan B: he created his own home studio located on the now-mythological Bellagio Road in Los Angeles, called back the rest of the Beach Boys, letting go of the session musicians he had previously deployed to record his hi-fi portents, and recorded a jagged, bizarre album on an eight-track recorder. The whole thing was done in a handful of weeks. It was raw and angular, even at its most bucolic. It ditched *Pet Sounds'* pristine production completely and abruptly. It was called *Smiley Smile*, a title both elated and menacing, like parted lips showing shiny teeth. A proper lo-fi record through and through.

Without even saying anything more on *Smiley Smile*, an enormous preliminary question must be settled: what kind of lo-fi is it? Why did Brian Wilson choose to leave hi-fi behind? From the looks of it, it would mostly seem like it wasn't something made with the conscious intent to sound the way it does. The poor recording was collateral damage caused by dire circumstances, the contractual siege of a hungry record label. Simply put, it was *lo-fi by mistake*. The actual *SMiLE*, the one that never was and that stalks the halls of *Smiley Smile*, was meant to be another *haute* hi-fi album like *Pet Sounds*, right? In many interviews and statements, both Brian Wilson and the rest of the Beach Boys repeated this idea: left to their own devices, the record would have sounded way different. They were forced to do it that way because they only had so much time to hand it in. Does our lo-fi story actually begin with a mistake?

Setting aside the revolutionary potential of *failing*, something that Jack Halberstam has explored extensively and that could be a great line of argument to defend the importance of something like *Smiley Smile* — a veritable glitch in the mainstream matrix stumbling its way unwanted to its global audience and failing to live up to the aesthetic norms of the capitalist world — I believe there's an even stronger argument. An argument that, quite banally, goes a little something like this: yes, *Smiley Smile* was a cop-out and circumstances forced Brian Wilson to go lo-fi, but it is actually not that far removed from what *SMiLE* was supposed to be. It is far from being a failure or a mistake! Its sound is quite organic to the experimentation Wilson was already working on in his studio seclusion, and it was only possible because he was already deeply fascinated with the potentials of *poor sounds*. And the evidence to back up this idea up is honestly quite extensive.

First and foremost, *Smiley Smile* is actually not the first Beach Boys' record that could be called somewhat lo-fi, or, probably more accurately, proto-lo-fi. In 1965, just before Wilson started his disquieting studio hesychasm, becoming familiar with radical soundscapes and the full potential of the means of music production, the Beach Boys had recorded an album called *Party!*. It was a fun little cover album, easy on the ear, leaving nothing much to write home about — aside, of course, from the many earworms that would immediately get stuck to the listener. The only remarkable quirk it had going for itself was that it was recorded as if it was a real beach party, background clamour and strummed acoustic guitars and occasional duds and all.

Take, for example, "Barbara Ann", the most famous single from the record. It starts with the band being aimlessly rowdy for a few seconds and then proceeds as if it was a spur-of-the-moment thing. People laugh in the background and hands clap sloppily throughout the chorus. The song ends with a few random reprises of the chorus with people talking and goofing around all over them. At its most surprising, as in songs like

"The Times Are A-Changing" or "I Should Have Known Better", *Party!* could easily fit in the back-catalogue of lo-fi labels like Woodsist. Of course, it was all "fake"; there was no party or, at the very least, no one actually invited you. But it's quite clear that the Beach Boys were already fascinated with what poor sounds could do: they could, for example, create a novel sense of intimacy, capture a dimension that hi-fi records couldn't even begin to fathom. Cheap sounds weren't *less* compared to the normality of high fidelity, they could easily be *more*. Deeper, more wonderous. If William Burroughs once claimed that the violent, raw sounds of an insurrection played in a crowd could actually create one, the Beach Boys understood that recreating the cheap echoes of a beach party could bring one into the privacy of the world's bedrooms and the listeners' ears. "There is nothing mystical about this operation. Riot sound effects can produce an actual riot in a riot situation. RECORDED POLICE WHISTLES WILL DRAW COPS. RECORDED GUNSHOTS, AND THEIR GUNS ARE OUT", and recorded party banter, and sandals and surfboards are out. Beneath the parquet, the beach! It just took the right sounds. It falls short from being our first lo-fi record mostly because of the way it uses lo-fi sounds as a cartoonish gimmick, but still, the fascination with poor sounds was already there.

Secondly, and more interestingly, *SMiLE* was always-already meant to be a record dotted with cheap and raw sounds from the very beginning, even before the terrible breakdown forced Wilson's hand to fully embrace lo-fi. We know, after all, that Brian Wilson had stumbled upon something quite radical in his studio experiments, something that in *SMiLE* should have taken its fullest, most accomplished form. But, thus far, we still haven't specified *what* exactly this experimental technique or set of unorthodox sounds that were fated to upend pop forever was meant to be. Simply put, when Wilson started envisioning what his next project was going to sound like, he had one clear insight into how he wanted it to be: a *modular* record. Plainly speaking, by modular recording he simply meant that the album was to be recorded using distinct modules, snippets of loose melodies, noise sequences and other strings of sounds reassembled together in the studio. Rather than writing the song as one coherent thing, he wanted to record bits and pieces to harmonize and contrast according to the sort of ambiance or flow they could create together, venturing outside the confines of the classical pop song and mimicking the patterns skirting by in a trip — physical or otherwise. A sort of sampladelic album, a precursor to the mesmerizing cut-ups of outer-folk acts like the Books and, more generally, sample-heavy music, from electronic music to trap, which would dominate the following decades.

He had already experimented with this style of sound-crafting, but now he wanted it to take over and become his sonic signature. This technique emancipated him from the strictures of the song-structure: he could make songs longer or shorter, symphonies or vignettes, according to their nature, and he could use unorthodox noises in them as long as they would somehow fit. He could also record them in disparate and just as unorthodox ways. His song could now be comprised of wildly heterogeneous things, free to clash or cooperate. It was, in other words, a way to collage together high and poor sounds, experimenting with varying degrees of raw and polish, artificially smashing against one another alongside tentatively strummed lonely ukulele, the most beautiful instrumental and the weirdest ambiance he could get on tape.

The most egregious example is what was meant to be the longest track on *SMiLE*, "Elements", a wildly experimental song about the four elements. The basic structure was meant to be quite odd: contrasting grooves interlocking into one another and, to give the listener a taste of the elemental, a barrage of noises, from the howling wind to water splashes and beyond. To record the part about fire, he forced the session musicians to come in with fire helmets on their head, a sort of shamanic play to evoke the fire spirits. He recorded a crackling fire, filling the studio with smoke and straining the recording process to its very limits. Of course, the fire in the building across the street broke out exactly while he was recording this precise bit. To the superstitiously inclined, make of this what you will.

Clearly, a modular recording does not equate to a lo-fi record. But it demonstrates something far more interesting: what made *SMiLE*'s recording process grand and baffling was Wilson's attempt to capture the totality of the sonorous spectrum, using sounds that the musical norm would often reject as waste. Tinkering directly with the machine made Wilson subvert his own ideas of how music could sound. Working solely in the studio, obsessing over the machinic technicalities of music recording, made him question how things are normally gone about. It gave him the ability to see the sorts of enclosures that compulsory hi-fi had forced upon music production and consumption and to trespass them — an act of direct escape through a sort of sonic hacking. He wanted to embrace everything that the pop machine could actually produce, profaning what was deemed acceptable and infesting his songs with banished materials. His sonicanalysis of the hidden reverse of pop music had led him straight into the realm of poor sounds and he found them, in and of themselves, a radical thing to use and explore, a way to set songs on fire and free them from their chains. This, of course, opened up the possibility of making, if need be, an entire record solely comprised of cheap sounds, the possibility of conceiving a fully lo-fi album.

These considerations have some interesting consequences, I believe, for anyone trying to grasp the revolutionary potential of lo-fi music. Namely, they dispel from the very get-go a certain image that has accompanied lo-fi throughout its existence, and that has somewhat contained and concealed this music's radical implications. Often, when talking about lo-fi, one can easily fall prey to a stereotype that describes it as a more "natural" music — organic, fully rid of artifice and mastery. Since it's more stripped back, it must be more immediate and naïve as well, the reasoning goes. A stereotype that could fit *Smiley Smile* like a glove: an album fascinating for its immediacy and rid of pompous studio tomfoolery. A band playing in the moment, no big studio in sight.

While, like most stereotypes, this might be true at times, it fails to capture the bigger picture, and the truly worthwhile thing to point out here: *Smiley Smile* and the lo-fi that followed in its wake is interesting because it points exactly in the opposite direction. In fact, Wilson's discovery of lo-fi sounds through his studio obsession, with his maniacal study of the technical minutiae of recorded music, was not a coincidence nor a contradiction: it proves, on the contrary, that lo-fi music is not any more "natural" than any other recorded sound. In reality, it is far more *artificial*, in the sense that it involves a practical analysis of the act of recording itself and the way it is done, today, under capitalism. The radicality of lo-fi music stems from the fact that, paradoxically, it blocks the natural recording flux, deconstructs its practices and conventions and uses all of those elements that were previously excluded to create something new and weirdly beautiful. The only thing that lo-fi seems to be "naturally" is *critical*, in the lesser pedantic sense of the term, but there's nothing natural in critique: critical practices bracket our most common mores, habits and customs and expose how everything, from the way we record our songs to the enormity of the capitalist world-system, is temporary, resting upon contingent material and historical conditions. Critique estranges its object to reveal how it came to be, to intensify the breaking points and escape routes. When Karl Marx obsessed in *Capital* over how a coat becomes a valuable commodity, it wasn't out of some masochistic type of fetishism, but to demonstrate how even the most banal of goods rests upon a substrate of processes that make it what it is. Or in more complex, Marxian terms, to show that: "the final pattern of economic relations as seen on the surface, in their real existence […] is very much different from, and indeed quite the reverse of, their inner but concealed essential pattern and the conception corresponding to it". Critique shows, in order words, the unspoken and hidden patterns that drive capitalist production. A lo-fi song, subverting the way a sound is normally made in the capitalist culture industry, similarly puts into question the conditions and the power-structures that shape it, the inner and essential patterns.

No need for any further messages or elaborations on top of the sounds themselves. The gesture of recording something in such a way is already an aesthetic affront and a political action in some very fundamental sense: it acts, almost like a parasite, on the material conditions of music production and opens them to new possibilities. Lo-fi is a critical form of art-making not because it adheres necessarily to this or that, but because it blatantly and directly questions and derails from within the motifs and the methods behind the most quotidian of sonic objects: the pop song. There's a great liberation in something recorded like shit. And who else could discover all of this other than someone who, more than anybody else at the time, immersed himself in the thick of the recording process? Someone who messed around with the mics, strings and cables? *Smiley Smile* was not a mistake then, but a more or less unforeseen consequence of taking back control of the music he made, discovering how and under what conditions it's made and exploring how many sounds a pop song could be made out of.

And the mere fact of recording something poorly, this peculiar critical practice, bears immediately its fruits on the overall conceptual themes and register of the thing recorded. In fact, the tone dramatically shifts in *Smiley Smile*. Gone is the duplicity, the thwarted run from this world that plagued *Pet Sounds*. The songs, despite being clearly moulded in Wilson's signature vision, are far more bizarre, artfully misshapen, than what we've ever heard on any other Beach Boys' record. The humongous hi-fi love songs and the sunshine frustrations that filled Wilson's most accomplished works up until that point are no more; now there's only the pure bliss of the sonorous equivalent of a Lewis Carroll or Russell Hoban story: dreamy, fable-like, fraught with psychedelic delights. It is a utopian record, in the sense Herbert Marcuse attached to the word: not as in "that which has 'no place' and cannot have any place in the historical universe", but as the liberation in sonic form of "that which is blocked from coming about by the power of the established societies". There are moments of sheer terror and claustrophobia, absolutely, but they're all part of the wonderous ride. And there's an experimental edge to the structure of the songs too: the way they strut or stumble or lurch forward; a characteristic that the stripped-down eight-track recording cranks up to 11. Most of the tracks sound like a pop song exploded in someone's living room.

Escape is, once again, one of the main themes of the record, but the grimaces and the captive double-entendres are a thing of the past. More often than not, escape appears accomplished — as something which has happened, successfully, at some point in time, as if the act of recording a lo-fi album had itself infused a newfound sense of freedom and hope in Wilson's poetics. The opening lines of the first song, "Heroes and Villains", a remnant of the *SMiLE* sessions that was completely made over and lo-fied in the process of recording *Smiley Smile*, speak volumes in this sense:

> *I've been in this town so long that back in the city*
> *I've been taken for lost and gone*
> *And unknown for a long, long time.*

We're out of bounds now. Objects in the rear-view mirror might be closer than they seem, but the universe of normal things has faded in the red dust of some uncharted desert.

One of the traits that will immediately pop out to a newbie's ear — or, at the very least, that surely put me off the first time around — is just how much Wilson *really* experiments with poor sounds on this album. A lot of the songs on *Smiley Smile* seem to be revolving around auditory trash, at least according to the industry gold standards. It feels lo-fi in every conceivable way, from the recording down to the very sounds spliced in the songs, to the point of being genuinely quite perplexing at times. Take, for example, the second track: "Vegetables". It starts off with a constant, pulsing thud grooving forward at full speed. The vocals immediately jump on top of the groove with a bunch of absurdist lines:

I'm gonna be round my vegetables
I'm gonna chow down my vegetables
I love you most of all
My favorite vege-table.

The narrator can't be located: the most probable guess on his whereabouts is some garden of earthly delights, or a cottagecore fever dream. As soon as the first verse ends, the voices quiet down in adorable harmony and something confounding blows up over the rest of the instruments: a wind instrument tooting like an owl. It is not entirely out of place, in a sense, amid the bumping rhythm, but slightly off-putting in its abruptness and dissonance. Kawaii plopping of water splashing in a glass washes over the song unannounced right after that, suspending the movement of the song. Some chaotic rustling, probably still coming from the glass or bottle, ensues and only then the song darts back on track with its irresistible thudding. All of this lasts just a handful of seconds, all wrapped in a slightly hissing recording. It is a labyrinthine experience, especially for someone expecting "Surfing USA".

On closer listen, it becomes obvious that the sonic madness is by design. The strange incursions, the improper sounds that erupt in the flow of the songs, are carefully sought after in an exploration of the potentials of cheap recordings. Thoroughly dispelling the myth of the naivety of lo-fi, Wilson clearly demonstrates that the weirdness of poor sounds is something that can be studied and consciously deployed as a voluntary means of subverting the normality of music production. An obvious example of this, egregious in its deliberateness, is

"With Me Tonight", a song that was aptly described by David Leaf in the liner notes of the record as "do it yourself acid casualty doo-wop". The song kicks off with the beatitude of harmonious glossolalia, the band chanting *On and on she go dumb bay do da* mindlessly, as if possessed by the most beautiful feeling in the world. No instrument accompanies the voices circling around the nonsensical mantra. Then, at the 0:26 mark, someone in the background breaks the placid repetition. He simply says *Good*, as someone would do after a satisfying take — something that would quite literally be the outer margin of any good pop song, destined to end up, naturally, on the cutting room floor. Did they forget to take it out in the rush to release the album? As Daniel Harrison noted in his analysis of the Beach Boys' experimentalism, this couldn't be further from the truth. On the contrary, the supposed dud interlocks perfectly with the rhythm of the song and marks a break in its overall structure, a break meant to make room for other harmonic lines to wriggle their way amidst the chant. It is an integral element left there for its auditory merits and its lingering radicality:

> While one might think that this is an editing mistake, it turns out that the control-room voice comes in exactly one beat after the singers conclude, and that it is delivered with a vocal richness that is itself musical and interesting.

It's in the song not in spite of, but by virtue of it being the epitome of poor sounds: lips smacking too close to the microphone with an unexpected richness, saying somewhat laconically the most banal of things. And the same goes for the rest of the clicking and clacking and splashing and all the other noises sprinkled throughout the album: they're there on purpose to break the bounds of pop, to hack it. It's all magical ephemera, from the paper-thin percussion punctuating the songs like fleeting ghosts to Mike Love's voice sped up to oblivion on "She's Going Bald", left where they stand wilfully, artificially even. Ephemera meant to disrupt and shine a light on another way of being and doing things.

"With Me Tonight" is interesting also on a thematic level, since it exemplifies what I mean when I say that escape is clearly a main theme on the album, but in an accomplished form. Wilson says very few intelligible things in the song. The lyrics simply go like this:

> *With me tonight I know you're with me tonight*
> *You're with me, tonight I know you're with me tonight*
> *For sure you're with me, tonight I'm sure you're with me*
> *tonight.*

In a sense, the song stands as the polar opposite of a "Wouldn't It Be Nice" or a "Caroline, No". There's no room for a hidden message, nor an untold, unrequited desire for anything more. He is sure that what he wants is either already here or will soon arrive. It's something acquired, not yearned. And who is he even talking about? A girl? An angel? It's truly irrelevant. The only thing that matters in the sparse lines is that there's this eternal teenage boy who finally got out, soundtracked by a questionably recorded doo-wop mantra. He sits at the edge of an ocean glimmering in the night with artificial fireflies cast on water by the oceanside city. He's sure he will never live through another dreadful Monday or endure a clammy commute to go get his life sucked out of him by some boss.

What seemed utopic for the neurotic narrator of *Pet Sounds'* hi-fi epic is now all here. A dream captured on an eight-track.

This, of course, does not mean that the ugliness of the world is forgotten, nor that it doesn't rear its hideous head from time to time. Nowhere is this more apparent than on "Gettin' Hungry". Again, this song seems like the absolute antithesis of another song from *Pet Sounds*, "I Just Wasn't Made for These Times". And just like that song, "Gettin' Hungry" gets dangerously close to being an openly anti-capitalist song. The narrator is hollowed-out by a dead-end job. *I wake up in the mornin' just to work all through the day*. The conditions which he has to accept are humiliating at best. *That sun can get so hot that you can sweat your strength away*. But right as the chorus starts, an invocation tears the scene asunder: *And oh, come the night-time...* The darkness of night, the physical embodiment of the multitudes that snuck out to enjoy their desires fully, cloaks the protagonist, and it alleviates the chokehold of the quotidian. Contrary to the desperation that stalked the guy from "I Just Wasn't Made for These Times", there's hope this time around. A hope that seems content in simply exhausting itself in the embrace of the heterosexual couple — *I'm hungry/Searchin' for a pretty girl* — without changing too much of the world outside, granted, but hope nonetheless. A hunger for a better life and some love to dismantle the sadness and impotence will do, for now.

The record fizzles out in a brilliant luminescence with an odd diptych, "Wonderful" and "Whistle In", doubling down on the lo-fi outsideness. In many ways, they are the summit of Wilson's experiments, the strangest of the bunch. "Wonderful" starts as a playful tune telling the tale of a girl in the woods. She's in the throes of a mystical experience, feeling the presence of a Great Outdoors as if all gates of enjoyment and freedom had broken loose:

She knew how to gather the forest when
God reached softly and moved her body.

The estrangement from the rest of the world now is total. There's the lingering sense that the liberatory trip is coming to an end, but not just yet. After a minute or so, the song implodes. Laughter and disjointed melodies ambush the listener from all around dementedly as the recording devolves in the poorest recesses of sound Wilson could muster out of those recording sessions. By the end of it, it has morphed into a little vanishing ambience where all bounds and limits get dissolved. Wilson whispers *wo-wo-wonderful*. The rawness of the sounds enhances the sense of aimless wonder. "Whistle In" then swoops in with offhanded whistling. It repeats over and over *remember the day, remember the night*, the time and place outside of the confines of drudgery.

After *Smiley Smile*, the Beach Boys surprisingly released a couple of other lo-fi records: *Wild Honey* and *20/20*. Sadly, they're both quite uninteresting. Stripped-down pop tunes and nothing more. Fun while they're on. Groovy at times, but the wild oddities and the grand melodies are gone completely. Brian Wilson had lost his grip on the band and the creative vein seemed bled dry. The only remarkable thing is the sense of exhaustion that oozes from them. The disquieting and extraordinary escapism lingers, but it appears ghost-like, ghastly and distorted by some other, much darker phantasmatic presences.

On a spring day in 1968, Dennis Wilson took up two hitchhikers, Ella Jo Bailey and Patricia Krenwinkel. They became friends and, for a while, they moved into Dennis's house on Sunset Boulevard with a rowdy bunch of people — a cult really, all revolving around a charismatic thirty-four-year-old man named Charles Manson. Manson wanted to be a rock 'n' roll star and convinced Dennis to let him record some demos in Brian's studio. The relationship between Dennis and Charles soon deteriorated. Nobody wanted those demos. Mason pulled a knife on Wilson and, in turn, Wilson stole a song from him. It was called "Cease to Exist" — Wilson renamed it "Never Learn to Love You". It appeared on *20/20*. It starts off with an ominous drone and then slides into a creepy love song about luring someone into ceasing their resistances and falling in love. For some reason, the stark contrast of the drone against the menacing pop song reminds me of one of the most extraordinary explorers of lo-fi darkness, Liz Harris and her project Grouper. A dark precursor of some sort to the darkest forms lo-fi would assume down the line.

In August 1969, Charles Manson sent Tex Watson, Susan Atkins, Linda Kasabian and Patricia Krenwinkel to what used to be Terry Melcher's mansion on Cielo Drive, a producer acquainted with the Beach Boys who had turned down Manson's demos. They did not find Melcher there, but they did slay five others nonetheless: Sharon Tate, Jay Sebring, Abigail Folger, Wojciech Frykowski and Steven Parent. The dream of an acid revolution died that night in the collective consciousness of the West, with "PIG" written in exsiccated blood on the mansion's walls. Or, at the very least, it started to wane irreversibly. It's hard not to think that the Beach Boys inherited that death, that they carried on their shoulders the mourning of a time when happiness was real, escape possible and revolution imminent. The only possible time that could have brought something like *Smiley Smile* to the world.

But Brian Wilson had managed to escape, at least once. In the face of the horrors and the horizons closing in, one record may not seem much, but even if the revolution got harder and harder to conceive and psychedelia was smeared with horrifying terrors, lo-fi was still there to stay and cause a stir. It was a sonic testimony that things could have been different, and still can be. Brian Wilson's fans are still assembling, to this day, uchronic albums made with his rough demos and studio outtakes, like the haunting *Trinidad Cassette*. They are ghosts of an escape that, for a split second, actually was; splinters from a universe in which it lasted forever. His lo-fi still shakes people out of the boundaries of normality. It leads them back to the dream of a world which could be free.

The ultimate underground

R. Stevie Moore and outsider glam

> *For anyone, anywhere, to have the same right to*
> *the same kind of stardom*
> Guy Debord

Artists are neat little things, aren't they? When looking at an artist's biography, especially of those canonically revered or blessed by a cult following, one usually finds a quaint order to it. A taste of intelligent design absent in anyone else's existence.

First off, you have a body of work: a concise or sprawling list of things this or that creative soul has put out into the world. Within this list, a progression or a repetition of certain themes and obsessions that ought to tell you who they've been and where they might go next. Sharp left turns can happen over the span of time, but people will complain or at least ponder on the reasons why they happened. Common people change their mind and their style all the time, but artists, especially when they have cracked the ceiling of stardom, don't. Their personality must be a tight grid that leaves little wiggle room: any deviation causes concerns and begs questions. A certain tidiness is expected to hold the personality together. Preferably, artists should be able to develop a personal signature and stick to it. Underneath the order of the body of work, a life just as fine-tuned: an existence of leisure or damnation, constant excess or torment. The sort of life that is so utterly out of our reach. Compared to them, we have the freedom to wake up at 3am wondering where we went wrong, wasting our days just being someone unremarkable. We are graced with voids and anonymity. An artist's life can have none of that.

Guy Debord spent insightful words on this predicament in his 1967 book, *The Society of the Spectacle*. According to him, the life of the performer, the artist and the star under capitalism was not an unconditioned biological event, briming with autonomous splendour. On the contrary, it was, as countless Žižek memes would have it, *pure ideology*, a representation that shapes the way we desire and live, actively ensuring the interests of the capitalist system overall. The artist and the star, in particular, according to Debord, function as machinery to keep the whole thing going, creating a phantasmatic image that both grinds for the survival of the chain of production and mystifies what actually happens to the humans that toil in its throes. "They" — the stars — "embody the inaccessible results of social labor by dramatizing the by-products of that labor which are magically projected above it as its ultimate goals: power and vacations — the decision-making and consumption that are at the beginning and the end of a process that is never questioned." Or, in simpler terms, the life of the stars serves both as something we should strive towards and never achieve — a life of limitless power and endless vacations — and a mask to conceal the various mechanisms of power and productivity. An *ought* and a *don't*, to gently entice you to desire this or that and make you oblivious of the material reasons why you can't get what you actually want. Artists, in the capitalist marketplace of ideas, are the imaginary means through which the quotidian, the normal, takes shape and keeps going.

Rather than lashing out at the stars with a slew of "how dare these artists force us to desire capitalism!", Debord takes a far more illuminating route. He immediately throws a provocation at us: precisely because the star is the mechanism that enforces what's normal and desirable, this "agent of the spectacle" is the least free of the social bunch. Sure, they're rich and famous, they're probably not as overworked and exhausted as the common folks, but they are the "opposite of an individual". Being the epitome of a successful person under capitalism, the star sacrifices their individual personhood altogether to become the blazing, lifeless effigy of those who have "made it". As soon as they step on the stage, they become "clearly the enemy of his own individuality as of the individuality of others". Mortified and then zombified, the artist puts its miraculous endeavours at work and forcefully chugs down their gullet the entirety of the value-system that underpins life under late-stage capitalism. Their life is so orderly and glamorous because they must become a commodity on a shelf: a clear label, transparent advertising, consistent with the brand. If they ever breakdown or decide to change entirely what they're doing, they still have to stuff it back into their persona somehow or get shunned into ridicule at the very least, if not straight-up obscurity. And this is a condition that — far from being rendered obsolete by the social media revolution, with its varied ecologies and fragmented viewerships — has been pushed to ridiculous heights now that everyone can easily become a niche internet micro-celebrity shaping the way a risible pocket of people think and act — behaving like rockstars did but with a hundredth of their power or influence. "Entering the spectacle as a model to be identified with, he renounces all autonomous qualities in order to identify himself with the general law of obedience to the flow of things." Won't somebody think of the megalomaniacs!

Provocations aside, the point is well taken: if we want to re-shape desire in us beyond capitalism, and since desire is moulded by what we are made to deem cool or sexy in our historical context, we must reclaim control over the tools that shape desire itself, stardom included. After all, as Marcuse clearly saw in his prophetic *Essay on Liberation* "What is now at stake are the needs themselves":

> the question is no longer: how can the individual satisfy his own needs without hurting others, but rather: how can he satisfy his needs without hurting himself, without reproducing, through his aspirations and satisfactions, his dependence on an exploitative apparatus which, in satisfying his needs, perpetuates his servitude?

We can't stop desiring or just scorn unilaterally the desire we are inhabited by right now. Saying "Fuck the Kardashians" will only get you so far. In a sense, as paradoxical as it may sound, it is true that we must free the stars, give them back their individuality, to regain more control over our ways of being and living. All glam to the people — but how?

R. Stevie Moore was born on a winter's day in 1952 in Nashville, Tennessee. A few years down the line, on another winter's day — his sixteenth birthday, to be exact — he was gifted a four-track reel-to-reel tape recorder. He was already a pretty skilled musician at that point, and so he started recording his little sketches and sonic intuitions right away.

He was extremely fond of the Beatles and, of course, Brian Wilson's Beach Boys — veritable obsessions of his — but also loved Jimi Hendrix and Frank Zappa. On that very special birthday, fate put him on the path of becoming one of lo-fi's most iconic and relevant figures, and one of pop's strangest, most improbable rockstars.

It would be impossible to craft a genealogy of lo-fi without R. Stevie Moore — he is, after all, possibly the biggest cult figure the movement has. "The original do-it-yourselfer", as he defined himself. But I think that his stature and idiosyncrasies are doubly relevant for anyone trying to grasp what is so radical about this way of making music, especially if we keep in mind Debord's provocation and the need to subvert the inhumanity of the popstar in the contemporary culture industry. What's so striking about his own personal trajectory and the meaning it took up for the lo-fi movement stems precisely from the fact that he deliberately wanted to be a star, against all odds and despite an absolute unwillingness to come to terms with any requirements to fit in. And when I say that he wanted to be a star, I don't mean it in a metaphorical sense: his music is enormous and flamboyant, despite being mostly recorded in the privacy of his home. It is so big it almost instantaneously proves a point: you can make the grandest pop music by your kitchen sink. His work is covered in the same stardust that fell upon Mark Bolan or David Bowie. And he was also obsessed with the largess of stardom as well: the money, the fame, the glamour. He truly wanted to be bigger than Jesus, in his own chaotic way — dodging any imposition or prerequisite to achieve that status. He was hellbent on never leaving behind his individuality and, in a sense, he did just that. He managed to show just how much could be achieved through a staunch lo-fi discipline, recording practically everything he did on his own with poor means. He wanted to: "be freed from the blackmail and the suffering of a forced labour that is already unnecessary and the enslavement to money", as Nanni Balestrini once wrote, something not even a rockstar can avoid under capitalism. He wanted to do away with the paltriness of normal sonic production and contemporary life in general, its "threatening homogeneity". No work and no boredom, only stardom!

This almost manic desire to become an unlikely, impossible star — while breaking off completely from the normality of pop and life under capitalism in general, which innervates all of his endeavours — is, in a sense, laid bare from the very get-go. If one was to check out his back-catalogue on Discogs, they would soon realise that this paradoxical artistic ethics is there in the very structure of his discography, if you could even call it that. It's right there in the way his body of work looks, even. Contrary to the order a pop star would impose themselves, releasing a discreet handful of albums, all clearly marked by some internal continuity or logic or glued together by the demands of the persona they would create for themselves at the expense of their human individuality, R. Stevie Moore would release everything he ever made on tape, chaotically and joyously and unapologetically. Untethered to the constraints of professional music-making and product-designing by a strict practice of home-recording, DIY-ing and genuinely not giving any fucks, he would turn anything he could get on tape into a record: this jingle he hummed on his lonesome one sunny afternoon, that Lennon-esque ballad so full of regret and pain, or that one time he stuck a microphone under a friend's nose as soon as he set foot in his doorway. Whatever came to him, every fleeting emotion was captured on the cheapest equipment he could get his hands on and immortalized for all eternity and for the enjoyment of every lovely weirdo in any corner of the world.

Everything would be worth a shot on one of his self-made cassettes, his main medium of self-expression. Nothing was too poor sounding, too meaningless or too erratic. Every single thing that his very peculiar individuality entailed could be recorded and included on an album. No artistic persona was needed outside of his own particular chaos. And he did not feel any ties or connections to any specific genre either. One day, he was a punk; the next, a noise musician or a sleek new waver. After all, who could prevent him from experimenting as much as he wanted to? The State? The marketing reps? In his basement, toiling on his tape recorder, he was free from all of that nonsense — practically escaping the demands of pop-capitalism through the practice of lo-fi, simply enjoying the abundance of his imagination and desire beyond any sort of scarcity.

R. Stevie Moore released more than four hundred records in the span of his life. The number varies according to the source you take into account. Probably not even Moore himself is exactly sure just how many there are. There will probably be many more on the day he departs from this earth of ours. He made so many albums and weird projects that no one will ever have the time to go through all of them, but the point was never to consume or sell them. They were made outside any market-logic, for the pure enjoyment of their existence as a document of a very specific moment in a very specific life. They exist not to become a commodity on our record shelves, but simply for the joy of existence for existence's sake, almost as a compulsion: "People tell me I'm shooting myself in the foot, releasing so much — I've heard that for years but I can't help it. It's who I am. I have this prodigy talent I was born with". "I have the ambition to release a new album every week", he would remark in a documentary about him, *Cool Daddio*. "I heard of overexposure, but this is ridiculous… well, I just wanna be rich", he would conclude, summing up his thirst for stardom and the walking artistic paradox he is.

The examples of this anarchic method of including everything there was to him at any given moment, without censorship or external constraints, are surely many. I am tempted to just say that all of his work is like that, letting you discover for yourself just how pervasively committed he was to the bit. But if I had to pinpoint my favourite moment of blissful chaos he managed to put on tape, I'd advise you to go listen to the first four tracks of his 1976 album *Phonography*, usually considered his first "official" album — meaning that it was the first to be released by a microscopic record company and not simply self-published like the rest of his early stuff.

Phonography kicks off with an almost prog-ish intro called "Melbourne": a grand symphony of a squeaky cheap synth, a guitar and some percussion, soaring in ways any Yes or Pink Floyd track simply couldn't. The song fizzles out in about three minutes and something appallingly different kicks into gear. A voice on its lonesome wonders: *What was that? Did you hear something?* The sound of someone justling in a bathtub and a knob turning in some shower somewhere in Tennessee. *Yes, it's me! I'm in the bathroom now and I'm going to tell you a little bit about myself as I bathe.* The tab starts crackling. *Robert Steven Moore is my name*, he clears his throat as you do when water and soap starts getting in your nose and your throat right next to the microphone. *I was born in 1952. January 18. I think it was about three in the afternoon. It was a Saturday that's for sure and ah…* This bathroom confessional, aptly titled "Explanation of Artist", ends before going anywhere and leaves the floor to a jangly piano tune soaked in recording hiss and echoes. A song all sunshine and imaginary saloons with tiny splashes of melancholia, again aptly titled "Goodbye Piano". At some point, he fucks something up while playing it and blurts out *Sorry*, leading the song to a chaotic falsetto-riddled ending, as if it was the most normal and natural thing to do on a pop album. Right after, another spoken word track: this time it's the "Explanation of Listener", a sort of interview given to an unnamed someone about living off the grid and creating communities. A kind of manifesto, without the loudness and obnoxiousness of a manifesto. The most surprising thing about all of this, however, is that none of it is filler or a bore. I guess it's just how an integral life functions on tape: anagraphical non-sequiturs, piano tunes and illuminations just flow in and out and there's no reason why they shouldn't stay on an album side by side. There's no dissonance, just the strangeness of actual existence as it is. The juxtaposition forcefully brings home the idea that that's what human individuality, in its fullness, sounds like in the form of a handful of pop songs — beyond the restrictions and personas built by market logic. It doesn't mean anything grand or totalizing; it just freely enjoys itself for what it appears to be at that very moment. Stripping away any overarching meaning and frustrating any attempt to assign some form of value to it, the songs exude something crucially splendid and banal about our human existence — something Gustave Flaubert saw better than anyone else: "You are doubtless like myself, you all have the same terrifying and tedious depths".

R. Stevie Moore was the son of Bob Moore, a shoeshine boy from East Nashville turned professional bass player. According to R. Stevie Moore, his dad inherited his musicianship, in a sense, from constantly shining the shoes of famous country bass players. He talks about his dad's rags-to-riches story as this almost mythical tale of a working-class boy absorbing the manners and skills of the ruling class. The part that he stresses the most, as if it was a dazzling miracle, is that his dad made it. He broke through to the mainstream. Bob lived his adult life proudly, almost boastfully, as a minor rock 'n' roll star. For ten years, his dad even played alongside Elvis Presley. He's the four strings behind "A Little Less Conversation" and "Viva Las Vegas". In the meantime, he was also a terrible father to the young R. Stevie. In many instances, R. Stevie Moore insisted that his passion for music came directly from him in a mixed bag of love and abuse. And, without psychoanalysing too much someone I only have a parasocial relation with, I believe that the mark of this paternal influence is plain to see in his work, both as the mould that would give his music its odd shape and as a sort of parricidal vein that runs deep in his weird endeavours. He lived in fear of his father, as if he was a looming black cloud over his existence on this planet, but he soaked in not only his love of music, but also that proud proximity to rock 'n' roll stardom — that thing R. Stevie Moore would work tirelessly towards in his own absurd way.

He would perfectly describe his relationship with his in a ballad eerily reminiscent of Brian Wilson at his most broken, "Father Goes". It is a song so soft that, at times, it sounds like a lullaby or curse constructed on a jagged acoustic guitar, angular vocal lines, chaotic drumming, echoes and synths. His father appears as a vanishing figure, constantly unloving and on the run. *That's where my father goes* repeats over and over, evoking both an aching absence and his dad's heroic escapades in the gilded world of the rockstars. Abuse seeps through in a few chilling verses:

That's where he can invent many problems
I can certainly tell
hearing him yell.

As the songs dies down, the silhouette of this broken and patriarchal relationship lingers. The father who played alongside Elvis Presley and hurt him so bad, God-like and untouchable in his brutal authority — an image R. Stevie Moore would bring up again and again in his songs and interviews — is a good encapsulation of the polarity that defines his sprawling body of work: R. Stevie Moore wanted to be a star, but he also wanted to end all of the sadness and loneliness and violence that life, be it of a rockstar or anyone else for that matter, demands under patriarchal capitalism. He wanted to be Elvis and murder him too. He desired, like all of us, all the good things that could eventually come from that soul-sucking process Guy Debord described in his analysis of the making of the stars, but with none of the pain and malaise and subjection and delusions of grandeur. R Stevie Moore has always been, throughout his life, a radical anti-authoritarian who aspired to all the grand things this existence of ours could offer. And he used a lifetime of lo-fi basement recordings as a weapon against the inhumanity of capitalist pop music — lo-fi as a means to transfigure pop into "the environment of an organism which is no longer capable of adapting to the competitive performances required for well-being under domination, no longer capable of tolerating the aggressiveness, brutality, and ugliness of the established way of life".

I say that lo-fi was a weapon to R. Stevie Moore almost in a literal sense because, as much as he tried to conceal his commitment to lo-fi recordings under a veneer of quaint slacking and sincere not caring, there's actually an underling combativeness to his almost monastic vow of sonic poverty. A political and aesthetic program, if you will. Despite his constant claiming that he chose lo-fi because it was simply the cheapest and easiest way to achieve his goal of making tons of records and, possibly, earning quite a bit of money as he did so — a motive we should definitely grant full credibility to — there's also something more to it: a certain propensity to sabotage normality as it stands right now and to conquer immediately and fully all of those things our capitalist society would concede only to the lucky few willing to sacrifice their existence to a life of toil and abnegation. Or, in other words, an attempt to escape the life prescribed by The Father Who Made It, a life of bending the knee (quite literally, in a shoeshine boy's case) and learning the ways of the ruling class in the hopes of being accepted into their gilded heavens. As much as he tried to sound dismissive, when it came to any ulterior motives to his lo-fi ethos — shield himself behind the idea that he was just a bedroom hermit who wanted to make music and make a lot of money without any effort — there's definitely a staunch, radical refusal of the aboveground world to his decision to ditch the normal way to go about producing a record. And, after all, isn't this quite apparent even in his dismissive defence of simply wanting to make a lot of money and albums as cheaply as humanly possible? Isn't this a confession of the desire to directly do without the judgement of any exterior institution that watches over and regulates the capitalist music industry? Isn't being just "a kid in his bedroom making music, getting close to 60 years old", quite a parricide already?

R. Stevie Moore wanted those gilded heavens, that glam that society affords to its stars, but he also wanted to make it accessible to the slackers and the losers and weirdos and everyone else. How else could someone like him break into the pop pantheon? And the only way to enact this radical program was, practically speaking, lo-fi: what other methods or ethos could be as effective in excluding any sort of authority from the pop productive process? Is there a more direct and immediate way to go about the total refusal of any discographic authority, other than simply choosing to do it poorly and unruly, with means that could potentially be available to an extremely wide audience? R. Stevie Moore's lo-fi is radical not because it consciously upheld this or that worldwide, but because it directly served as a method to contest how things are in this peculiar historical conjunction, just as Guattari predicted when talking about radios and his adolescent son. A loaded gun to the heart of all aesthetic authorities. Lo-fi gave him the power to steal the fire from the hands of the star and give it to the rest of humanity. "If he could do it, you can do it too", was the message. In the wake of R. Stevie Moore, no gods, masters or record labels could stop you from becoming a basement rockstar, whoever you are. Glam to the people then, through lo-fi.

Even on a merely biographical level, his lo-fi solidified itself as R. Stevie Moore's signature style through a soft parricide. After a period spent working in his father's studio, R. Stevie Moore decided to leave his hometown. His father wanted him to follow in his footsteps, stay in Nashville and become a session musician for some country or rock 'n' roll big shot. But in 1978, he decided to turn his back on his father's dream to become something that could stand on its own two legs. At twenty-five, he relocated to Montclair, New Jersey. There, something quite dazzling came his way: punk rock. For the first time, he was exposed to a style of rock 'n' roll that stepped outside of Elvis Presley's imposing shadow, and an underworld of rock heroes that had nothing to do with what his dad taught him. These bands banged the drums and drew blood with their six strings, but they did it in ways that were completely unorthodox and counterintuitive. He loved the Sex Pistols, a band capable of embodying the shape of glam to come, rotten and new. They were, after all, just as larger-than-life as his father's music, but sleazier — closer to a sensibility that came from some untamed and wild Outside. He got obsessed with darker stuff as well. He liked post-punk's sounds of enmity. He loved Public Image Ltd., for example, with their haunted minimalism, their tireless industrial mania. And in turn, the New Jersey punks reciprocated his love. By then, he had already recorded quite a bit of music. He had even put out *Phonography*, that first "official" studio record. The punks he met there were among the first to get his weird music — an amazing achievement for someone whose music was ostensibly far weirder than any punk rock or post-punk. They made him a sort of local star. In New Jersey, he had his first fan club, as he'd always dreamt of, as small and informal as it might have been. And he was not rich as he had hoped to be, surely. He was clearly no Johnny Rotten or Joe Strummer. But someone really understood him for the first time — the first members of the invisible legion of those who would find something inspiring or even life-changing in his work; a demographic that would eventually grow and grow over time. "I showed up in New Jersey right when punk was hitting, and I was an instant celebrity. I bleached my hair and I spiked it out, and I was Johnny Rotten from hillbilly land. It was so innocent then, total lo-fi", he would later recall.

The conceptual upshots one could extract from R. Stevie Moore's lo-fi are a quite few. First and foremost, with

R. Stevie Moore and his parricidal style we actually see, in a sense, the real birth of lo-fi proper as a movement and a style, and we can start to gauge at its radical nature in its fullest form. This, of course, does not imply that Brian Wilson's lo-fi (or Paul McCartney's, Lou Reed's, Bruce Springsteen's, etc.) were lesser forms, or less interesting musical experiments overall. But they were all virtuous forerunners coming from within the industry itself. Brian Wilson's lo-fi, as we've seen, was already a parricide and a revolt in some major senses, but he was also someone fleeing from the capitalist aesthetic norm while being fully enmeshed in it. It was an imperfect revolt, still embryonal. R. Stevie Moore, on the contrary, was always an absolute outsider — even taking into account his proximity and troubled relationship with his dad-star. He did not belong to the aboveground world, and he never wanted to. His absurd stardom did not imply any form of compliance whatsoever. With him, a radical option was born, or the very least, it was fully consolidated: choosing escape from the get-go, choosing lo-fi as the sole means to communicate one's artistic vision. In plainer terms, lo-fi became an *actual thing* — an almost-genre characterised by a constant conflict with the polished universe of capitalist pop music. A kind of punk more punk than any other punk. Thus, R. Stevie Moore truly is the father of something quite unique: a sort of *outsider glam*. Something almost unheard-of before his sonic adventures. Something that would be an inspiration for the entirety of the lo-fi movement as it stands today. After R. Stevie Moore, everyone had a good antecedent to deliberately choose to be unmarketable, completely sincere, maybe a little unhinged. Everyone had the right to an outsider glam that belongs to "the common beyond and beneath — before and before — enclosure", to the undercommons. In a sense, he invented or, speaking one's mind. Nature is not in it; its real source is primarily technical. It is not something one gains from simply going with the flow; it's a positive freedom that must be practiced on a very pragmatic level. It is a set of mannerisms and practical decisions necessary in order to express the profoundness of one's banal existence in an aesthetic form beyond what normality dictates — a quotidian depth that, in turn, we are probably unable to confront in its proper essence without these same mediations, tricks and mediums. As Maurice Blanchot once put it: "the immediate is not close; it is not close to what is close to us. It staggers us". Sincerity is a style in the most arid and austere of terms: it is, first and foremost, a conscious way of handling the tools of the trade in one way rather than another. R. Stevie Moore's outsider glam shows that the expression of an integral existence beyond the current restrictions and impositions must pass through an upheaval and subversion not only of the things one says, but also and more fundamentally of how and through which mediums the thing itself is said. It entails working like a mole on the machinic subconscious of our artistic expression.

The medium truly is the message, after all, and saying more objective or truthful things is not what R. Stevie Moore's lo-fi sincerity was about. And indeed, a lot of the time he does sing about extremely inane or absurd things, completely detached from the cold facts of the real world. The point of R. Stevie Moore's sincerity was, first and foremost, the active overturning of how a pop song is made. If properly understood, then, his lo-fi and sincerity go hand in hand, and do not imply a regaining of naivety, but a loss of many of our aesthetic habits in favour of a scathing practical critique of how we things normally go about things. Both sincerity and lo-fi, then, are a de-habituation, a reweirding of our usual ways of making art and expressing ourselves. Lo-fi, understood as a way to record everything without any exterior control with the cheapest possible means, entails the discovery that the productive process that shapes a song is not an extrinsic element, untethered from the contents expressed in the song itself. It also implies the insight that, without a practical critique of the way the means of sonic production shape the limits and forms that a feeling and a life assume within the bounds of a pop song, nothing really radical can emerge. Lo-fi, rather than a being a naïve, immediate genre, as the stereotype would have it, proves itself to be, once again, a practical critique of how songs are normally made on a very down-to-earth, technical level. Lo-fi equates to an obsession and a constant messing with the machines, the hidden reverse of pop music. It's a luddite sabotage that breaks the habitual, mute function of the machines. And only through this machinic sabotage can sincerity gain a radical significance.

To put it briefly, if R. Stevie Moore did not consciously decide to refuse the studio-industrial complex all his life, he would have probably produced a very different type of music, in a starkly different quantity and with very different meanings and messages. Without a direct, almost militant intervention within the material conditions of music production, he would have lost his voice, his singular individuality. His trademark sincerity would have been unfathomable without the methodical use of lo-fi as a way to hack and take control of the various practices that create a pop song. And even if we were to interpret his style as a mechanical consequence of his slacking or "total innocence", as he'd like us to, it would be a mechanical choice with great consequences for his craft nonetheless. The shape of his discography, so adverse to any sort of market-logic, is only possible because lo-fi technically permits a radical new way of going about the production of a track — it liberates many possibilities that the overseers of the making of the commodity and its value-form would prefer to block, suppress and render unthinkable. And this perfectly mirrors Brian Wilson's obsession with the studio and his subsequent discovery of lo-fi, but from a perspective of radical outsideness: only through a real confrontation with the machines, an intimate relationship with the way they work, can a new form of expression emerge. R. Stevie Moore chose sonic poverty, and precisely from this choice descends the structural features of his work and his unbridled sincerity.

And his attack on the normality of pop production did not stop at the recording process either. When he started to gain a few fans up in New Jersey, an issue arose: how to distribute his tapes. For someone who wanted to cut out any sort of exterior authority, this sort of logistical problem was everything but a secondary issue. After all, letting someone else market his records meant giving up the power he had so strenuously fought for. It would have entailed alienating his individuality in favour of some persona or marketing ploy that would fit some label's bill — conceding to some outer structure the right to create an artificial image of his art in order to deliver it to his fans' doorsteps and sell it to potential new buyers. Again, the material relations were the thing he had to tinker with and subvert if he wanted to maintain power over his craft and preserve his uncanny sincerity. "Power is" indeed "logistics", as the French insurrectionists of the Invisible Committee once proclaimed. He had to find, in other words, an equivalent to the directness and effectiveness of the lo-fi method when it came to sending tapes to his fans, precisely because lo-fi as a method to hack the normality of pop production had granted him the material space to freely express himself, a space he

This very loneliness, this achingly personal struggle against a monster too big to be defeated, proved itself to be R. Stevie Moore's worst demon throughout his life, and the biggest limit to the radicality of lo-fi as a strategy deployed to exclude any sort of exterior influence. Despite his loyal fan club, R. Stevie Moore never got the recognition and wealth he actually aspired to. His grandeur and his desire to become some sort of weird John Lennon in the eyes of the world were always a one-sided affair: the vast majority of people had no idea who he was. My mom and dad have no idea who he even is, and yours probably don't either. He often claimed to be "suicidally depressed" over the so-called arc of his "career". "I'm still bitter, and I'm still waiting for recognition" would become a sort of mantra when talking about how his artistic trajectory turned out. He felt like he was good for nothing. He suffered immensely because he felt relegated to the liminal edges of the culture industry. A lonely hillbilly exiled in some province of the music biz. An unlovable child, forever. In a sense, his situation mirrored perfectly the one described on the Beach Boys' "I Just Wasn't Made for These Times": a lonely man completely out of place in the hideous capitalist grind, without any real, solid community to back him up.

And from a disgustingly cynical perspective, one could ask: what did he expect? Did he really believe he would make it without complying to any of the demands of the society he was living in? His music was badly recorded in an almost militant, guerrilla-like way. His discography was wilfully unmanageable and unmarketable. He presented himself as a weirdo. There's no way he could have made it. He often voiced this sneering, depressive inner voice in his own music too. Take, for example, one of his most famous songs, "Part of the Problem". In a sense, this is the quintessential R. Stevie always fell inwards, never outwards. He always considered himself a failure and never openly criticized the systemic ostracization that most weirdos of any sort and variety suffer at the hands of the inhuman star-making process Debord so clearly theorized. He was always fundamentally a no-good, it was always his fault. He seemingly never considered his exclusion a political and impersonal affair, something that could have been undone through the abolition of the material conditions that structure the aesthetic realm under capitalism. His loneliness was never tied to the contingent nature of how the world is today — something that will very likely end or, at the very least, change in the not-so-distant future — but an immutable feature of his being. His depression was his, and his alone. His solitude was an ontological fact. He never explicitly took up the idea that a phrase like "one is not the kind of person who can fulfil roles which are earmarked for the dominant group" has always been a political construct devised by the ruling class in order to keep people like him (the weirdos, the misfits, the deviants) in check and regulate that which can be said and desired. The radical insight, so clearly expressed by Mark Fisher, is that the "sneering 'inner' voice" that characterizes a depression like the one experienced and narrated by R. Stevie Moore is not "an 'inner' voice at all — it is the internalised expression of actual social forces, some of which have a vested interest in denying any connection between depression and politics." This is something that would have probably explicitly politicized his music. It could have led him to consider his exclusion from the riches of the stars as a political matter, rooted in the radical refusal of the very idea that some are destined to have a persona and a revolting amount of money and others are just going to be unknown consumers. It is the final destitution of The Father

Who Made It, the ultimate parricide. The paradox at the heart of his outsider glam turned against him and revealed its dark side: he totally refused to play by the rules, but he succumbed to the values he had internalized.

This blind spot in R. Stevie Moore's radicality sheds an interesting light on the argument we have been weaving thus far: the idea that lo-fi is a form of practical critique that undermines the pop-productive process through a direct hacking of the machines. Considering R. Stevie Moore's loneliness, one question seems unavoidable: is it enough? Are Guattari's pirate radios, or even Radio Alice for that matter, that effective at the end of the day? As radicals, we have to face again and again the same problem in our analysis of this or that countercultural phenomenon: capitalism is still standing, after all. What appears clearer than ever is that, without an honest yearning for a communal struggle, any escape from normality is bound to be an ineffective quest, both on a wider, social scale but also on a more private, existential one. Lo-fi can, like in Moore's case, show us a way to break down the tools of the rockstars and make them our own, but without a genuine collective yearning for that other, psychedelic world that pressed, alien, unnameable and immaculate, against Brian Wilson's lo-fi escapades, this might end up being a sterile endeavour. Messing with the machines on your lonesome may give you some invaluable breakthroughs and newfound forms of expression, but without a desire to collectively transvaluate all this world's values, to truly break out of it, this sabotage is doomed to be neutered and neutralized.

But a community grew nonetheless out of R. Stevie Moore. His music planted the seed for what would become the lo-fi movement as we know it today. His staunch refusal of anything tidy or polished made it possible for others to experiment with rawness, ugliness, sincerity; to try and launch some sort of attack on the studio-industrial complex and liberate sounds that were considered pure trash. As he himself sang on one of his most anthemic songs, "The Winner", his position as an absolute loser would in the end turn out to be a victory of some sort:

> *Who is the man doing everything he can*
> *The winner the winner*
> *At the finish line first one every time*
> *The winner the winner*
> *He spends his life in a box*
> *Of ideas he can use*
> *But every night you can find him alone*
> *A loser.*

He may not have found the success or recognition he was looking for, but without him we would have probably never witnessed MGMT's or Mac DeMarco's or Ariel Pink's rise to indie stardom. He made it possible for them to be rockstars in their own unlikely way, for better or for worse. The wave of lo-fi that swept the global underground in the 2010s would have never been a thing if it wasn't for R. Stevie Moore's trailblazing. And glam would have been more exclusive, more homogenous, if he had never disseminated his odd tapes across the world. He may not know it, but he made Guy Debord a little proud.

ours, we've lost the maximalist sense of the absoluteness of evil they so outspokenly championed. For us, evil is something punctual: a death, an illness, a stroke of bad luck. Or, for the more politically inclined, it's a regime or a political structure or some tragic social event like a war. For a lot of our contemporaries — and I'd be even inclined to say: the vast majority of our contemporaries — the sky is relatively empty of divinity and bad things are relative to very worldly occurrences. It's rare to meet somehow who downright blames the Devil for their misfortunes today — it's truly a noteworthy and unique event, something at least I would find quite startling. But Frank and Ida Mae Hammond certainly did believe so. And if they were right and the Devil does exist, we certainly are underestimating his dominion over this world.

They expressed their belief most fiercely in their book *Pigs in Parlour*. The tome sold well, at least according to their Wikipedia page, and it is vicious, almost venomous. It is spiteful, belligerent. From the very beginning, they make absolutely clear their stance on evil: "Much is being written today on this subject of demons", they initially concede, but "few have dealt extensively with the practical aspects of deliverance from demon spirits". To them, we're unprepared soldiers on a battlefield we can barely even see. Our own bodies are microscopic battlefields desecrated by unclean spirits on a daily basis: "Demon spirits can invade and indwell human bodies. It is their objective to do so". Their list of symptoms that render these invasions manifest is basically all-encompassing: emotional problems, mental problems, speech problems, sex problems (which, of course, boils down to all non-heteronormative behaviours), addictions, physical infirmities, religious errors (of any degree, they specify). Everything that strays even slightly outside their narrow definition of goodness is a battle scar. And people should arise and embrace the struggle: "This book is [...] a trumpet call to total spiritual warfare".

The thing that is possibly most striking, if not downright disturbing, about the book is its political scope. When we think about deliverance from evil, our mind often wanders to the ordeals of private exorcisms: Regan MacNeil crawling down the stairs like a spider, Emily Rose contorting maniacally, and so forth. Frank and Ida Mae Hammond, on the contrary, believed that deliverance was a social affair. Individuals were infested by demons not out of some personal guilt, but because society overall was sick and perverted. "The Church and the individual believer must get beyond the concept of personal deliverances to the concept of spiritual warfare against the spiritual potentates who are called 'the spiritual hosts of wickedness in heavenly places' (Ephesians 6:12)." Theirs was a vicious political theology. The grace of God had to be enforced through radical social change. A deeply reactionary and brutal social change, but a social change nonetheless.

Of course, the politicization of religion is nothing new. Every religious institution in the history of humanity has acted as a political agent, in one sense or another. But the interesting thing about Frank and Ida Mae Hammond is the fact that theirs is an expression of what could be vaguely considered a sort of American folkloric religiosity, often based in Christianity but not exclusively, encompassing all sorts of magical thought, which has had an undeniable influence on quite a few people — whether through the embrace of this sort of faith or from passing cultural exposure.

These sort of belief systems are certainly not a peaceful or private affair, but a spirituality often aggressively oppositional to the rest of the world. Taking Christianity, the Hammond's professed faith, as a meter to assess the nature of their beliefs, they're evidently quite far from the stuffiness and abstractness of the more institutionalized churches of the old continent, and they speak to a "we", a congregation, that is often quite loose and formless. Their goal towards this patchwork of heterogenous believers is to directly help them in their struggles, right here and right now — even or especially if it means condemning the whole of society and inciting some sort of political action. Like many televangelists, preachers and sect leaders, they don't speak with the assurance of a consolidated dogma or with the outspoken benevolence of an official Church, but they present themselves as charismatic guides in a wretched world and their authority stems from an unmediated reading of the Bible and the Gospel that is quite naïve, practical and direct. And quite dangerous, indeed. They have problems to solve and demons to fight and the ills of modernity to squander; they have no time for the airy conjecture regarding the Holy Trinity or stuff like that. There's no room for doctrinal marginalia. It is a spirituality characterized, first and foremost, by militancy, warfare, conflict. In their extremity, Frank and Ida Mae Hammond are a good exemplification of a sort of spirituality which has thrived under many guises in the hyper-aggressive climate of contemporary capitalist America, and which has had quite a bit of influence over this world of ours — sometimes in milder and gentler strains, sometimes in monstrous forms, incarnated in malignant crooks like Jimmy Swaggart. A network of faiths, mutually excluding each other, but all hellbent on changing your existence rather than discussing what God's actually like.

Daniel Johnston, a key figure of the lo-fi movement, was one example of this sort of spirituality. He was born religious and he remained that way, but he was not really invested in any Church. He grew his own ethics to save his soul. He had no relation with the Hammonds either, at least as far as I know, but his beliefs, too, were practical and militant rather than doctrinal. And his art and his radicality are utterly incomprehensible without giving central stage to his own spiritual warfare — his will to escape this world and find a place where the utmost Good shines through. While R. Stevie Moore's escape was motived by worldly desires (becoming a star by breaking all the rules), Daniel Johnston strived for something more: an alien joy, something quite divine. He was a sort of DIY gnostic, if you will, convinced that this world is evil and that it should be fled. His was a political theology as well. He cultivated his own special kind of magical thinking to fight a world brutal and desperate. Luckily for our genealogy — clearly a partisan endeavour, clearly anti-capitalist — he was no reactionary: the dominion of evil coincided, for him, with the ugliness of capitalism, not the degeneracy of modernity. His Church had three unshakeable pillars: Evil, Hope and Love. Evil is everything boring and meaningless capitalism subjects us to; Hope is the undying assurance of a way out; Love is the struggle to escape. And I'd say that his theology, with its three pillars, coincided almost perfectly with one of the most interesting forms of contemporary anti-capitalist thought — a form of anti-capitalism that Mark Fisher has called "acid communism".

Just as in R. Stevie Moore's case, it would be outright unthinkable to even begin to sketch the significance of lo-fi without including Daniel Johnston. If R. Stevie Moore was the father of the movement, the one who made this sort of paradoxical form of rockstarship fathomable, Daniel Johnston was the poster boy for the genre. His body of work is the perfect incarnation of what lo-fi would look like for decades.

His album covers were the perfect visual embodiment of the movement — rough, black-and-white, filled with this air of mysterious, almost jarring naivety — and his songs were the very first introduction to the charms of poor sounds for many people, including a number of very influential musicians and artists, belonging to both under- and aboveground scenes. Kurt Cobain famously wore a t-shirt dawning the front cover of one of his most famous albums, *Hi, How Are You?*, and everyone and their grannies has covered one track of his or another, from Spacemen 3 all the way to Lana Del Rey. To many, Daniel Johnston and his very peculiar poetics were the very first exposure to the world of lo-fi proper and its will-to-escape.

As otherworldly as it may be, the origins of his faith are easy to pin down. He was born in 1961, the youngest of five. His father was an engineer who fought in the Second World War as a plane pilot. His parents were very religious. On his official website, in the About section, they're openly described as "a Christian fundamentalist household". They belonged to a non-denominational church called the Churches of Christ. For the uninitiated, a non-denominational church simply means that the congregation does not recognize the authority of a traditional denominational church. Their beliefs are rooted in the Bible and the Gospel, but they do not subscribe to the dogmas of any of the main churches. The Churches of Christ, in particular, are a group of heterogenous congregations, with varying degrees of differences and disagreements among themselves, which recognize each other as like-minded Christians. Or as they put it: "Each congregation of the churches of Christ is autonomous, and it is the Word of God that unites us into One Faith". They have "no central headquarters or president" since, well, "The head of the church is none other than Jesus Christ".

Nonetheless, I'd say that his Christian upbringing is not the only source of his own peculiar taste for the divine and the mythic. After all, throughout his life, Johnston was not straightforwardly Christian, even though some, if not most of the references of his weird political theology came from Christian culture. His sense of the sacred also stemmed from a personal, wide-eyed consumption of what I'd call, loosely following Roland Barthes, "capitalist mythology". According to Barthes, myths are simply "a type of speech" and anything can be a myth since "the universe is infinitely fertile with suggestions". Of course, this implies that capitalist culture has almost necessarily produced many myths, with which it makes sense of itself and ensures its continual survival. Still, according to him, the biggest myth of all today is certainly the stories and the depictions that the ruling class has been weaving for themselves for its relatively brief existence. After all, it's fairly obvious that the bourgeoisie truly created an eternalizing mythology to either hide or justify its existence and power. It has painted itself as the "social class that does not want to be named", creating both the narratives that there either is no ruling class at all under capitalism or that its power is simply a plain fact of nature, unmoving like the law of gravity: "The status of the bourgeoisie is particular, historical; man as represented by it is universal, eternal". In simpler terms, the most important myth of all under capitalism is that the elite cannot exist and, even if it does, it cannot be overthrown. But there are also many other lesser myths under capitalism: Superman or Batman, John Wayne or Ronald Regan, Ronald McDonald or the Wendy's Twitter account. All of these are, in a sense, mythological creatures, with their distinct speech-forms, narrative arcs and their prodigious or nefarious deeds. They are probably not as integral to capitalism as the myth of the eternal or non-existent bourgeoise, but they do create a web of tales that grants a meaning and sense of shared community to our capitalist society. And the young Daniel Johnston would find extraordinary insights in some of these capitalist myths, insights that would inform the pillars of his own faith. His spirituality was a syncretic belief system that hybridized the teachings of Jesus Christ with the things he'd see on TV or hear on the radio.

The myth that lit his heart the most, the one that inspired him to give music a try, was certainly that of the Beatles. He was veritably possessed by religious fervour when it came to the Fab Four — a truly peculiar possession, given Johnston's hyper-religious background. After all, the Beatles were veritably the Devil for the American Christian right. But to him, they were a manifestation of something higher than this world, true mythical creatures walking the Earth with the rest of us. He loved none just as much. "When I was 19, I wanted to be the Beatles. I was disappointed when I found out I couldn't sing", he'd say. In 1984, he released a song titled after them that would prove just how profound his faith was. Like most of his songs from that period, the recording is quite raw and the sole accompaniment to his nasal, urchinular voice is a cheap piano. It kicks off by comparing the minute fact of his own birth with a much grander event, at least to him: the Beatles' first singles.

> *When I was born in '61*
> *They already had a hit.*

He then goes on to sing their deeds, as you'd do with Ulysses or Achilles:

> *They worked so hard and they*
> *Made it too*
> *They really were very good*
> *They deserved all their success*
> *They earned it yes they did they didn't*
> *Buy their respect.*

And the song ends immortalizing their grandeur, highlighting just how mythical they seemed to Johnston:

> *Like history now to read*
> *Like a magical fairy tale that's hard to believe.*

If not bigger than Jesus, they truly were just as big to him.

The Beatles, though, were not the only myth that would capture his imagination and fervour. There were others that were also probably more interesting on a doctrinal level, so to speak. Some came from Marvel comics — Captain America, for example. These comics endowed him with a taste for the great mythological battles of Good and Evil, the just versus the greedy and the crooked. But there were also odder ones, more leftfield. For example, still in 1984, he released a song dedicated to Casper the Friendly Ghost. And as paradoxical as it may sound, it's hard to imagine a better introduction to his own peculiar political theology — to the escape he was plotting from this tiresome world.

Casper, in Daniel Johnston's song, is a figure of pure Goodness, nailed to his own insecurities and short-comings, on the run from a world he could not conform to. A figure that would become a veritable archetype of his poetics. Casper provides to Johnston a saintly image of worldly holiness which he describes in naïve, lullaby-esque lines:

He was smiling through his own personal hell
Dropped his last dime in a wishing well
But he was hoping too close and then he fell
Now he's Casper the Friendly Ghost.

The personal hell Johnston talks about is not some vague eternal damnation, but a very real, tangible feature of Casper's earthly existence: even though he's a kind soul, he's considered lazy — he can't be just as productive as the rest of society and meet capitalism's demands:

He was always polite to the people who'd tell him
That he was nothing but a lazy bum.

Death, in such a world, is Casper's escape, and a productive one at that, at least according to Johnston:

Nobody treated him nice while he was alive
You can't buy no respect like the librarian said, but
Everybody respects the dead, they
Love a friendly ghost
And now they say we'll never forget what he learned
As we were mean to him but he never burned
Just singing, "love lives forever!"

Leaving this world behind let's some love shine through, breaking the wheels of the quotidian that were grinding poor Casper. As funny as it may sound, to Johnston, Casper the Friendly Ghost's myth was a source of Hope for an existence without Evil and a demonstration that Love, the act of struggling and escaping the grasp of this world, always wins.

Just like R. Stevie Moore, one of the key features of Johnston's song-writing was an unbridled, radical sincerity. He would sing about things that would normally be excluded from any respectable pop record — they were too up-close-and-personal, at times too unhinged. He would speak of love, death and faith in terms far too candid for the music industry. Compared to R. Stevie Moore, the tone and theme were, nonetheless, starkly different: while R. Stevie Moore developed a histrionic stream-of-consciousness splattered through a sprawling discography, Daniel Johnston was far more restrained and, like St. Augustine, way more confessional. He almost exclusively focused on documenting the trials and tribulations of his faith and his life in a world in which he did not belong — his cosmic teen revolt against existence under capitalism. But just as in R. Stevie Moore's and Brian Wilson's case, his sincerity, his radical escape from any market-logic and aesthetic norm, boiled down to a matter of practical subversions. The means through which he recorded his first tapes — a now legendary $59.00 Sanyo boombox — allowed him to hijack the machinic mediations that produce a "normal" pop song, hacking them to his advantage. Once again, his sincerity presented itself as a technical by-product of lo-fi as a method. Through lo-fi, he could record whatever he wanted without the stuffy restraints of the studio. The communion with his Sanyo boombox gave him full control over his own expression, freeing him from the demands of the industry. Once again, lo-fi manifested itself as a practical critique of how things go normally about — an immediate, radical gesture. Lo-fi gave his weirdness a chance to explode unconstrained.

According to Johnston himself, he started composing music at an impressively young age. When he was nine, he started toying around with his first compositions. But it wasn't until the early Eighties when he started recording his first proper tapes. He enrolled in an art school at Kent State University. He wasn't very invested in the academic life; he didn't care for the classes there and his heart surely wasn't in what he was being taught. He had a lot of time to kill. In the meantime, something else happened that completely changed the course of his life: he fell in love with a girl named Laurie. He became obsessed with her. His love was not reciprocated at all. She was already engaged to a local undertaker. In the opener of his first album, "Grievances", he even says that he met her at a funeral home where her partner was working. She was collecting coats and as soon as she said hi to him, he was struck down by an immense feeling for her, too big to describe. Once he confessed:

> a lot of my songs are about funeral homes. I always quote it. It's all the same. Once I had that song I went from there. There was this girl, and I wrote this song, "I Love Inkles" or something, and I played it for her on the piano at the university and she said "gee, you do that well" and that's all it took. Every day after that I was sitting at the piano going bum-bum-bum. I never really stopped. Then I got this song "Grievances" and they all refer to that song.

He would later recount the whole story, in and of itself the stuff of legend in all its vaguely grotesque charm, in obscenely honest detail in one of his most beautiful songs, titled, of course, "Laurie". This sad, goofy story would also go on to

us to tears and rips the fabric of the cosmos. It was true for Daniel Johnston.

The mark of this angelic love is deeply felt in his first two albums, *Songs of Pain* and *More Songs of Pain*. Most of the lyrics are sung, as you might expect, in a lowkey evangelical tone. He often sounds like a zany, caricatural prophet, or something like that. Songs like "A Little Story" are literal retellings of humanity's original sin and the crucifixion of Christ, just to give you an idea of the scope of his bizarre political theology. At one point, at the tail-end of "Joy Without Pleasure", he even jokes about the song being a sermon against premarital sex, poking fun at his own religious inclinations and postures. The majority of the tracks are the unlikely parables of a man stranded and loveless in a world whose demands he'll never meet. No love, no job, no fun. The girl who left opened up a wound that irreparably tore the fabric of the world. The lack of love, its slipping away, is a portmanteau of the scarcities of this joyless world, chock full of nine-to-fives and obligations and no fun at all. This everyman, just like Jesus Christ, is innocent and martyred by an Evil world: told he does not belong, refused by his one true love, forced into a life of unemployment and misery. The protagonist of these songs has surely found Love for a little while, a breach in the order of this dreary existence, and has become an unlikely messenger of its wonders, but he has to confront the fact that the powers that be (earthly, like bosses and parents, or otherworldly, like fate itself) are hellbent on forcing him into a life devoid of real pleasure. He realizes that his happiness has always been horribly thwarted on a personal and social level, even before his first heartbreak. He's moved by Hope, as Daniel Johnston's gospel commends, but he has to confront the reality, and banality, of Evil — be it an unrequited love or, more often than not, generalizing his sadness and frustrations, the meaninglessness that capitalism subjects everyone to.

Johnston's most anthemic song in this regard is "Joy Without Pleasure", the aforementioned anti-premarital sex track. First and foremost, it sticks out for that very pun: superimposing a theological and conservative message at the end of a song that is neither of those things, he highlights the general tone of his poetic. The joke makes his bizarre posture not just visible, but downright obvious. In a peculiarly meta moment, he makes the weirdness of his ideas and his music manifest. He speaks like a preacher, his lyrics read like something straight out of some sermon, and he sings like a kid in his parent's basement recording his shaky voice on a boombox. Have you ever heard anything like that before? The distaste for this world that the song radiates is clearly something that has to do with a broader spirituality, a set of personal dogmas — a distinct vision of the Good and the Divine that makes this world quite unbearable. A faith sung by the strangest preacher of all.

Secondly, and most importantly, this song clearly unites the personal vicissitudes of Johnston's life to a social malaise that afflicts everyone under capitalism. It is an anti-capitalist song that takes Johnston's particular experience as a sort of social paradigm that could be extended to everyone living at this historic conjunction. The track is clearly sung from the perspective of a heartbroken man. Laurie is never explicitly mentioned in any which way, but the protagonist is certainly not happy and quite lost. In the first half of the song, the lyrics present to the listener a young Daniel Johnston. He's a confused child who cannot understand what's right or wrong. He's the living image of pure innocence, the perfect ambassador for his anti-world (and, in turn, anti-capitalist) mysticism. His life, full of impotence and young frustrations, becomes his own spiritual and critical archetype. A sense of sullen powerlessness creeps in with each verse:

> *When I was a little kid*
> *And all the people, they looked big*
> *I never exactly understood*
> *How to tell the tree from the wood.*

The song immediately segues into the chorus, which lays out the whole point:

> *Joy without pleasure*
> *Ain't no fun, ain't no fun at all.*

The narrative that underpins all of Johnston's theology is laid bare in this simple words. Just like in Captain America, Casper the Friendly Ghost or the Gospel, there are two competing forces: Good and Evil. Joy sits on the side of Evil and it is a portmanteau of all the satisfaction one could possibly gain from living by the rules of this world. Pleasure, on the other hand, stands firmly with the Good. It is the longing for an escape, for a true and proper love. Once again, we find a definite set of values: Evil, which means boredom and complacency, and Love, which is the struggle to be properly free and desire whatever one's heart desires. Hope is yet to make an appearance, and the song is, as you'll see, quite bleak. But it lingers in the background, as always.

Love notwithstanding, Evil and its manifestation on Earth are far too big for someone this innocent and young and lonely. Can a boy overthrow all worldly boredom by himself? Of course not. This discomforting fact is voiced by Johnston's mother, who, right in the middle of the song, sketches the silhouette of Evil: working in a factory until your hands and your brain are numb, just to barely get by each month. Simply put, working for a boss under capitalism:

> *My Mama, she took me aside one day*
> *She said "you better have fun while you play"*
> *'Cause someday you'll wake up and you'll be old*
> *And all of your youth will be gone away*
> *And you'll work in a factory and earn your pay*
> *And your fingers will rot and your mind will decay*
> *You'll be happy, so happy, with your family and house*
> *But you'll never, you'll never enjoy yourself.*

Life under capitalism bars real enjoyment from everyday life. Its satisfactions are mere ghosts of fulfilled desires. Love can only shine, as a sort of alien creature, through child's play, reckless abandon, absolute infatuation. Or, in other words, as Marcuse put it in *Eros and Civilization*, while the joys of capitalism are ordered and enclosed by a restrictive "performance principle", which shapes all desire as competitive and productive desire, real pleasure follows "a higher form of reason", the main feature of which is the "very negation" of the sad passions of sane productivity: "receptivity, contemplation, enjoyment".

> Behind the definition of the subject in terms of
> the ever transcending and productive activity
> of the ego lies the image of the redemption of
> the ego [...] The purity, regularity, cleanliness,

> and reproduction required by the performance
> principle are not naturally those of any mature
> civilization. And the reactivation of prehistoric
> and childhood wishes and attitudes is not
> necessarily regression; it may well be the opposite
> — proximity to a happiness that has always been
> the repressed promise of a better future.

The song ends diverting its radical critique of capitalism's bleak joys — it's about premarital sex, after all — but the redemption Marcuse wrote about is the same Daniel Johnston fervidly believed in. Love is fighting for this repressed promise beyond production and capitalist reality. Hope is knowing it's a real thing.

This is precisely the intersection where acid communism and Daniel Johnston's political theology undoubtably meet. When writing his fragment on acid communism, published posthumously after his untimely death, Mark Fisher was going through a period of political optimism, mostly fuelled by a critical recuperation of Marcuse's "great refusal of capitalist reality". Fisher believed that there were powerful insights to be unearthed in that sort of psychedelic thought. In fact, the "acid" in acid communism did not refer to LSD at all, but it indexed a recuperation of that "concrete utopianism" that underpinned Marcuse's critique of capitalist enclosures. According to Fisher, "the great refusal rejected, not only capitalist realism, but 'realism' as such", producing "a 'rational negation' of the existing order of things". It was "acid" because this sort of post-capitalist politics hinged around an ecstatic recuperation of a concrete politics beyond the grey impositions of capitalist economy and the entirety of its reality — just like Daniel Johnston's political theology implicitly implied.

Capitalism, thought Fisher and Marcuse, had reached a point in history where it had become technically useless, and even harmful. Its restrictions and enclosures of all common goods and pleasures were there just to keep people from revolting against its needless drudgery. Furthermore, the capitalist economy produced real scarcity by endlessly pillaging the natural resources necessary for infinite consumption. "Capitalism", according to both Fisher and Marcuse, is an economic system that "generates artificial scarcity in order to produce real scarcity". By which they meant, in simpler terms, that capitalism creates, on one hand, artificial enclosures that regulate how much people can actually satisfy their needs and enjoy their lives and, on the other, wastefully consumes the means to satisfy those same needs. It forces people to live with their hunger for no reason other than keeping them in check and, simultaneously, squanders environments and resources and lives without equitably redistributing those same resources to all who need them. Fisher and Marcuse elaborate on this insight by letting us glimpse the end of this economic system: "Actual scarcity — scarcity of natural resources", after all, "now haunts capital, as the Real that its fantasy of infinite expansion must work overtime to repress", while "the artificial scarcity […] is necessary, as Marcuse says, in order to distract us from the immanent possibility of freedom". Capitalism might collapse sooner than we can imagine.

The upside to this possible collapse is surely the idea that hunger, boredom and all the other unpleasantries that capitalism produces on a mass scale, both directly and collaterally, could be, technically speaking, eradicated — if only the mode of production and distribution of wealth were forced to run otherwise, of course. This meant, for Fisher and Marcuse, that the revolution was both attainable and desirable. Hope, as Johnston clearly saw, was a feeling to be cultivated because it was well grounded in the actual reality of our contemporary economic system. But it also meant, in turn, that, in order to keep that same revolution at bay, capitalism would be forced for the rest of its existence to keep on privatizing and depriving us of all unproductive joys: fun, play, love and all the other gateway drugs to capitalism's beautiful extinction. *Joy without pleasure ain't no fun at all*, sung Daniel Johnston, but pleasureless joy was and is necessary to dispel the spectre of a world which could be free.

And the idea that an artist, oblivious to anything Marcuse-related, could practically be an acid communist in their aesthetic practices was an eventuality that Fisher and Marcuse absolutely endorsed. "Art was", for both Fisher and Marcuse "a positive alienation", something that could strip us of all our habitual attachments to capitalist reality. While "His Frankfurt School predecessor, Theodor Adorno", said Fisher, "invited [us] to endlessly examine the wounds of a damaged life under capital". By contrast, Marcuse vividly evokes, as an immediate prospect, a world totally transformed". Art was, for Marcuse, a veritable rupture that materialized utopia in the present. A breather from how the world actually is and an insight into how it could be. Art is, therefore, for an acid communist, a time-machine beyond the present or a direct point of contact with other worlds. The only characteristic that an artist should manifest to be an acid communist is a certain familiarity with "a laughter that comes from the outside. It is a psychedelic laughter, a laughter that — far from confirming or validating the values of any status quo — exposes the bizarreness, the inconsistency, of what had been taken for common sense".

Acid communist art had to be the voice of "some anonymous X, a faceless being". And Daniel Johnston's weird religious sensibility is nothing but a laughter coming from the outside: his gnostic conviction that this world is Evil and that Hope and Love exposed a way out of it all surely unearthed a kind of pleasure that had nothing to do with this reality of ours. His gospel was an acid communism because it negated the greyness engulfing us, letting something else, something other, something yet unnamed shine through.

In the early Eighties, Daniel Johnston moved to Texas, where he lived for the rest of his life. He lived with one of his brothers in Houston at first. There something happened, something akin to R. Stevie Moore's experience in New Jersey: he got recognized. He finally found a crowd. MTV even dedicated a now infamous episode to this bizarre music scene in its program *The Cutting Edge*. His name was starting to circulate in the then blooming indie scene. By the 1990s, he had become a sort of unsung hero of the American underground.

As he got more and more famous in the Houston scene, he also became the protégé of an up-and-coming noise act that would dedicate a lot of time and energy in making his art flourish: the Butthole Surfers. He wouldn't even dare to say their name out loud out of childish embarrassment. He'd call them the B-Surfers. But they truly got his weirdness. They saw something in his DIY pop tunes. And he even found himself a manager, Jeff Tartakov. The relationship with him was quite troubled, to be honest. But all of these people helped him find a label interested in his stuff, to break out of his ultimate underground and have a shot at the mainstream. The two main competitors for his music were none other than Elektra and Atlantic Records. He chose Atlantic in the end. Elektra had signed Metallica and, to him, they were a satanic band. He didn't want to be near the devil's acolytes at all. He only recorded one album for Atlantic, *Fun*. It was produced by the Butthole Surfers' guitarist Paul Leary. He had already dropped his manager. He wasn't made for this world. His improbable breakthrough into the mainstream music scene never was.

His bright Texas days also coincided with a new understanding of Evil. He had his first experiences with LSD, a substance that revealed itself to be, as in Brian Wilson's case, both angelic and demonic. After his encounter with Laurie, this was his second breakthrough encounter with an alien reality that tore the fibres of this world of ours asunder. He felt as if he had awaken, had touched a deeper layer of reality where he could test first-hand the veracity of his theological dogmas. He could see the battle between Good and Evil raging on directly. His mental health was deteriorating as well. LSD could not remove the Evil he fought against and the clearer vision he thought it granted him also came with a sharper, colder form of pain. The material conditions of his life could not change like that and the pain and loneliness that haunted him could not be removed by turning on, tuning in and dropping out. The Human Operating System (OS), as Mark Fisher once defined all the systems of control and political subjugation that enclose our everyday life, remains unshaken in front of the occasional chemical transgression: "a display of that Romantic fetishization of self-destruction" is, more often than not, "far from being subversive or transgressive". It may very well be "the Human OS in person". If not extended and properly realized by a communal movement capable of abolishing the present state of things, drug-induced psychedelia remains a mute insight of the repressed promise of a better future. This, for Johnston and Fisher, was the dark underbelly of acid communism.

There's one recording of Daniel Johnston talking to Gibby Haines of the Butthole Surfers about his experiments with LSD. It is quite a precious document of his glorious breakthroughs and cold paranoias. In it, Johnston speaks in a feverish tone, almost maniacally. He is probably high, but that's wholly irrelevant. A dick and swastika loom behind him like black, imposing clouds. He goes back and forth between anguish and elation. First, he explains the meaning of one of his most famous song, "Walking the Cow". He says that "walking the cow" means carrying the weight of the world, bearing your own cross. It is a terrifying image, blurted out at rapid-fire speed. He immediately moves on: he says he is awakened, unlike most people. He sees the world as it is and he knows what's right and what's wrong. "It's like a comic book." He saw, he keeps repeating, he saw. He then goes on to explain his paranoid ideations: he feels like he's being watched by Evil forces. The Government, The Law, The Media, The Top 30 Radio: all agents of Evil, all out to get him. He describes a Coca-Cola mind-control experiment and a military coup that was bound to happen over Christmas. He also talks of Hope and salvation. He could be saved, he says, if only he could put all his heart in his art. If only he could be as free from Evil as he'd like to be. Acid was all of those things for him: persecution and salvation, downfall and ascent.

In 1990, Johnston had his most severe breakdown. His dad was flying a two-seater plane out of Houston. He had just played a music festival there. His dad was bringing him to West Virginia. He was sitting there, reading a Casper the Friendly Ghost comic book. In the strips, Casper falls from the sky with a parachute to get out of danger. To the hypomanic

Daniel Johnston, this was a profound story of redemption. He himself felt just like Casper, one of his personal images of sainthood, and like Casper he had to fall out of danger. He ripped the ignition keys out of their slot. He threw them out of the window. The plane fell out of the sky. It crash-landed, blown to bits. "There was nothing down there but trees", recalled his father after the fact. In the documentary *The Devil and Daniel Johnston*, there's a scene where "there is a photograph of them taken just after they emerged from the forest, standing in front of a billboard outside a country church. It reads, 'God promises a safe landing, but not a calm voyage'. In Daniel Johnston's mind, this was further proof that Jesus was winning out over Satan in the long and torturous battle for his soul". The billboard was from the Church of Christ, Daniel Johnston's family congregation.

This period of revelations and breakdowns was not wasted on him. It brought Daniel Johnston to recording his most accomplished album, *1990* — the most complete, delicate exposition of his weird theology. A proper lo-fi masterpiece.

The album is doused in this strange esotericism; it's full of cyphers and codes that can only be unlocked through a full comprehension of Johnston's personal spiritual warfare, his private dogmas and his fraught existence. It recapitulates all of his pains and joys and desires. It sketches the eternal battle between Evil and Love, and Hope's undying longing.

1990 was meant to be Daniel Johnston's first proper studio album. Just like his previous one, *Continued Story*. His manager had put him in contact with Sonic Youth's Steve Shelley, who invited him to New York to record in a real studio. He got there in April, 1988. He was meant to stay there only a short while, playing a few gigs and finishing the record in a couple of weeks or so. He stayed there much longer. At one point, he got "arrested for drawing the Christian fish symbol all over the Statue of Liberty". During his concerts, he would erupt with sermons about the reality of Evil, the eternal struggle of Love and the divine grace of Hope. The plan to record a "normal" studio album fell through. The final product is a mix of the studio recording sessions and home recordings.

Even on a merely technical level, the album is quite interesting. In a sense, it proves the point that lo-fi acts as a material sabotage, which liberates new ways of expression. *1990* lacks the composure of the albums Daniel Johnston actually managed to record in a studio, especially *Fun*. And in more than one sense, *Fun* is a better album: more consistent, easier to enjoy, less erratic. But the themes and sounds are also less *personal*, for lack of a better word. It's not less sincere, in the strict sense of the word; he still speaks his mind freely and it's evidently a Daniel Johnston album through and through. It's chock full of God and acid and Captain America and Laurie references, after all. But there's a constraint to everything about *Fun*. The act of completing *1990* with home recordings creates an evident difference between the two projects: in both he is sincere, he's always clearly speaking his mind, but in *1990* the more or less wilful act of sabotaging the studio process creates spaces where freer expression can actually happen. It's not a matter of what he says, it's the technical methods he uses to record what he's saying that makes all the difference. Lo-fi, once again, is not more naïve or direct or whatever else the stereotype would have it to be; it's a practical critique of the material conditions of sonic production, which enables forms of expression that are normally censored or excluded. It's direct action, like the anarchists would say, on the machinic unconscious of pop.

The album begins with two real depictions of hell, which are among some of Johnston's more paranoid and terrifying descriptions of Evil: "Devil Town" and "Spirit World Rising". The first is a brief, soft song. His voice stands alone with no backing instrumentation. It describes the whole world, but Texas in particular, as the devil's town. Everyone around him is a vampire, living under Satan's dominion. He's a vampire too, corrupted by his guilt and sins:

> *I was living in a devil town*
> *Didn't know it was a devil town*
> *Oh Lord, it really brings me down about the devil town*
> *And all my friends were vampires*
> *Didn't know they were vampires*
> *Turns out I was a vampire myself in the devil town.*

This world as it stands is simply Evil and must be combatted. Spiritual warfare is the only way in Daniel Johnston's political theology.

"Spirit World Rising" picks up from this bleak vision, blowing it up to apocalyptic proportions. *The devil has Texas*, he repeats over and over. Everyone bears *The number on their forehead and hands*, referencing the Mark of the Beast described in Revelations 13:16. But right as the song begins to fade, divine intervention strikes, introducing the positive element in his theological belief system, his weapons in this battle against this horrid world:

> *From the sky the number seven*
> *The devil defeated*
> *In the sky the New Jerusalem.*

There's Hope and there's a battle to be fought.

After this thorough exposition of the first dogma, the album moves on to the second with two thematically interlocking songs: "Held the Hand" and "Lord Give Me Hope". They're both prayers, really. They are both a confession of guilt, acts of penance to gain reassurance in a way out. "Held the Hand" is a simple prayer. Johnston asks God to forgive him for having held the hand of the Devil. He has succumbed to earthly boredom, which, interestingly enough, for Johnston, is the Devil's clearest calling card, as if the time you spend in an office numbing your mind and soul were the surest way to earn eternal damnation. He then goes on lamenting that he has been on MTV too, another agent of Evil he embraced. He asks forgiveness for Laurie too, creepily enough. "Lord Give Me Hope" is a more complex prayer. It's a chant about the longing for Hope, a certainty in a way out. Daniel Johnston's a sinner and living in this world is tough. Normality is a burden to carry, the cross everyone has to bear on top of their own private Golgotha. Everything about this existence of ours is unbearable for such an alien creature:

> *Lord, give me hope*
> *For the road*
> *I walk upon*
> *The road, it is long*
> *And I fear*
> *Lord, give me strength*
> *For my burden is great*
> *And the road it is long*
> *And I'm afraid.*

But this despair serves only to make Hope more apparent. Anguish is the black light that shows the reality of a way out:

> *I know you are the one*
> *The one and only door*
> *Take my broken heart*
> *Make me whole again.*

A total abolition of everything that stands is a not a mirage, it's a palpable reality. An outside that presses against the dreariness of all our insides. The fight for our souls must be fought reassured that all of this is temporary:

> *Christ, guide me now*
> *To do what is right*
> *Show me the truth*
> *And to win the fight.*

Then comes the third dogma, the most combative of all: Love. It comes in a triptych. The first part is "Some Things Last a Long Time", possibly the best song about being lovesick ever recorded. It's, of course, about Laurie:

Your picture
Is still
On my wall.

Love is not an easy feeling; it's an obsessive intruder. It derails normality. It is an aberrant intensity that does not respect the tidy performance principle that keeps this world together:

The colors are bright
Bright as ever
The red is strong
The blue is true.

It haunts, stalks. But it's hard not to perceive Johnston's sentimental militancy: he believes in love eternal, a fiery principle. Laurie's blue coincides with everything true, otherworldly. Love transfigures life, and even its absence and violence make the Earth liveable:

Things that we did
All we forget
Some things last a life time.

The second song, "Tears Stupid Tears", extends this unruly Love and makes it an active engine for Johnston's gnostic mysticism. Love still haunts on this track. Those tears, stupid tears, bring him down constantly, like gravity. But they are also a disruptive force. They expose just how lacking this world is. Tears are a revolt:

I was born in the body and right from the start
Those tears, stupid tears, been tearing us apart.

From the very moment he got incarnated into this world, tears sprung as a rip in the fabric of existence. As they flow, they shed a new light on what it means to be at all and to be in our current historical conjunction. According to Daniel Johnston, as painful it may sound, we must accept the intensity of lovesick tears. Simone Weil would agree:

> I should not love my suffering because it is useful. I should love it because it is […] We have to say like Ivan Karamazov that nothing can make up for a single tear from a single child, and yet to accept all tears and the nameless horrors which are beyond tears. We have to accept these things, not in so far as they bring compensations with them, but in themselves.

This intense, heart-shattering cavalcade ends with a call to arms: "Don't Play Cards with Satan". In it, Johnston lays out the basic principle of his spiritual war tactics: don't get near Evil. Its industries, its organizations, whatever has to do with his boredom and drudgery must be fled. Escape is the only viable option out of this predicament. And Love, in its proper sense, is just that: escaping Evil's long, dark tentacles. Otherwise, *he'll deal you an awful hand*.

The album peaks with "True Love Will Find You in the End". It's Johnston's go-to song for every neophyte. On the face of it, it sounds like a simple love song. It revolves around the promise of true love:

> *True love will find you in the end*
> *You'll find out just who was your friend*
> *Don't be sad, I know you will*

But don't give up until
True love will find you in the end.

There's a catch to this promise, though:

Only if you're looking
Can it find you.

Love is real and it is looking for you. But Love can only be a struggle to get out of here, moved by the undying Hope in a better future. You will have to look for it with all of your heart and soul. But there's a better life out there, outside capitalist reality. There's an outside untainted by sorrow. That's a promise. In a doctrinal sense, the song wrapsup all his political theology: the misery we all endure, the fight to end it, the assurance in a real, better tomorrow.

In September 2019, Daniel Johnston died of natural causes. He was only fifty-eight years old. As he departed from this world, an outpouring of love flooded my social media. Everyone who ever felt like an outsider, at one point or another, was mourning the loss of his bizarre holiness. Contrary to R. Stevie Moore, he never buckled under the cross we have to mount on our shoulders just for existing in this precise historical contingency. With him, lo-fi's technical sabotage was paired with the intensity of a life spent for love and hope. His radical fervour, his lovesick extremism, was clearly agitated by "the spectre of a world which could be free", a world where capitalist normality could be no more.

Mark Fisher, while sketching out the features of the enemy of all acid communists and post-capitalists, defined neoliberalism as an exorcism of this very spectre that moved Daniel Johnston's political theology:

the overcoming of capital has to be fundamentally based on the simple insight that, far from being about "wealth creation", capital necessarily and always blocks the production of common wealth. The principal, though by no means the sole, agent involved in the exorcism of the spectre of a world which could be free is the project that has been called neoliberalism.

As someone who saw this very exorcism as the Devil's deed, Daniel Johnston truly stands as lo-fi's chief acid communist.

Photographs of long
weekends by the sea ·

Marine Girls and the politics of oceanic feeling

"Woman" is that which the "male" unknows of himself.
Heriberto Yépez

In 1977, Klaus Theweleit published a strange book. A tome
of outer psychoanalysis. It was called *Male Fantasies* and it
dealt with a sinister subject: the unconscious dreamworld
of the German Freikorps. The Freikorps were, as Barbara
Ehrenreich explains in her precise introduction, "the volunteer
armies that fought, and to a large extent, triumphed over, the
revolutionary German working class in the years immediately
after World War I". In other words, the Freikorps were the
armed forces who, led by Rudolf Höss, brought Adolf Hitler
to power. Given their monstrous endeavours, Theweleit tried
to investigate the desires that ruled these men. Their evil
was puzzling to him; he wanted to understand what kind of
pleasures, fears and complexes dwelled in the innermost part
of their psyche. Were they monsters? What did they dream
of? Did they cherish the bloodshed? Did power turn them
on? What kept such men awake at night? Were they afraid
of violence? He'd plunge in their diaries, their confessions

and their proclamations to see what kind of unconscious is a Nazi's unconscious.

The underlining thesis of his psychoanalysis was both fascinating and terrifying: the Freikorps had nothing special going on for them. They were just people, like you and I, and their unconscious did not hide any special malignity. The only real difference, according to Theweleit, was that they had formed a particularly vicious way to express their desires through the practice of war and power. For Theweleit, they were simply an extremely aberrant instance of the chasm between sex, death and power we experience in each and every one of us. After all, we know propaganda and the ballot box turns us on, in some sense. Haven't we all been in the heat of a political argument before? And everything is about sex, aside from sex, which is about power, isn't it? The same political excitation that runs through us ran through those men, but in that historical conjunction it led them to the most horrifying of outcomes, the most brutal extremity. In short, they craved power, power excited them, like it excites us, albeit in hopefully different and far less genocidal ways.

If this thesis was correct, if the Freikorps' desire was no different from our "normal" one, then only one question remained to be solved according to Theweleit: Can we recognize the symptoms of such a desire? After all, if it happened once, it could easily happen again. Unless we sketch a thorough profile of the pleasures and phobias of the Nazis, we won't be able to see it coming when it will eventually rear its ugly head up again in our friends, neighbours, lovers. Exploring their unconscious became for him an ethical imperative. Or as Ehrenreich, again, puts it:

What is far worse, Theweleit forces us to acknowledge, these acts of fascist terror spring from irreducible human desire. Then the question we have to ask about fascism becomes: How does human desire — or the ceaseless motion of "desiring production," as the radical psychoanalytic theorists Deleuze and Guattari call it — lend itself to the production of death?

The portrait of Nazi desire that Theweleit managed to paint is, admittedly, quite wonky. Sometimes he goes on and on about this or that feature of their unconscious, basing his analysis on what amounts to anecdotical evidence and analytical stretches. I'd say that most of the book is far more fascinating as a pulp novel with some really gruesome details, rather than an actual psychological study. Nonetheless, scientific validity aside, as is often the case with pulp novels, the most gruesome bits hide some very interesting speculative insights on the things we find sexy or revolting. One such instance is, I believe, Theweleit's fixation with a very specific Nazi phobia: thalassophobia.

According to Theweleit, the Freikorps men had an indomitable fear of open waters. The roots of this fear, still according to him, were a strictly gendered thing: while the Nazi men wanted to be solid, muscular, impenetrable, the unbound seas stood as a fluid mass, endlessly formless and ever open to penetrations of all sorts. Water's oceanic feeling represented the twofold terror of penetration and of all those people who crave being penetrated. Water was a sort of psychic stand-in for an omnicidal form of feminine desire, a desire that everyone could harbour within themselves, no matter what gender they were assigned at birth. A desire diametrically opposed to the masculinity and solidity they so fiercely clung onto. A savage, psychedelic ego-loss. As Theweleit puts it:

> The person is split into an inner realm, concealing a "numbly glowing, fluid ocean" and other dangers; and a restraining external shell, the muscle armor, which contains the inner realm the way a cauldron contains boiling soup. Writers have seldom given names to the streams in and on which desires flow toward unknown human futures. They are oceans, rivers, springs, surges, or simply waters, the endless movement of this matter without form.

They lusted over things controlled, possessed, enclosed: the ocean is none of those things. The Nazi's psychic ocean was chaotic and open. Sometimes, it was politically revolutionary. In fact, Theweleit claims that his thalassophobic Nazis would even describe Bolshevism and the global surge of socialist politics with aquatic metaphors: "The wave of Bolshevism surged onward, threatening not only to swallow up the republics of Estonia and Latvia, neither of which had yet awakened to a life of its own, but also to inundate the eastern border of Germany", writes Wolfram von Oertzen on the Baltic situation at the end of 1918. Bolshevism seems to be a kind of ocean that surges onward in waves, inundating and engulfing. Wherever the "Red flood" — also the title of a novel by Wilhelm Weigand, about the Munich socialist republic — was sighted, the cry of "Land under!" pierced the air. "The Reds inundated the land".

As it's fairly plain to see, whether this analysis is correct, or even provable, is wholly uninteresting. And, probably, it's simply not the point. Some Nazis might have feared the open waters because they unconsciously dreaded this unbridled, feminine ego-loss, sure, but it's evidently quite hard to scientifically prove and, at the end of the day, the fascinating side of Theweleit's analysis is certainly not its analytical capabilities. On the contrary, its power stems from the fact that it's a magnific story that evokes and deconstructs some psychic images hardwired in our gendered desires: masculinity as solidity, landlocked, hard and impermeable to otherness, and femininity as radical openness. It's a myth, just like Casper or Captain America were for Daniel Johnston, which we can use to dissect our innermost lives, acting upon them as a society and as individuals. It's telling, after all, just how deep the roots of this story run in psychoanalysis: just to name the most famous ones: Freud himself, in the twenty letters, exchanged with the French mystic Romain Rolland, and in *Civilization and its Discontents,* confronted, albeit quite pessimistically, the terrors and grandeur of the "oceanic feeling", a term he borrowed from Rolland himself to index the psychological experience of ego-loss,; one of the foundational texts of early psychoanalysis, *Thalassa* by Sandor Ferenczi, more explicitly deals with this troubling marine unconscious to explain human sexuation and the birth of our innermost desires.

None of these images, of course, are grounded in any solid reality, and it's probably best not to take them too seriously: there's no biological destiny that binds any of us either to masculinity or femininity, nor masculinity to some land-being and femininity to some sea-essence. They are all clearly just spectres of our neuroses and dreams. And they work quite well when it comes to making us feel uneasy, shaking the habitual.

They're mere parables and, as Jackie Wang has suggested in *Oceanic Feeling and Communist Affect*, we can deploy them to attack heterosexist masculinity and the capitalist organization of desire as a whole. They can serve as a starting point to embrace a radical form of pleasure, being and political action. Our "marine unconscious" is simply a fairy-tale, good for analysing phenomena which might resonate with this fascinating articulation of human desire. Just like Marcuse's haunting promise of a better future, the oceanic feeling could not be "an infantile defense or regressive return to a pre-Oedipal state" — as Freud, someone who claimed he never experienced any such thing, would have it — "but part of a mature process of becoming; an experience of ego loss that enables one to commune with the 'substance' of existence in a way that radically alters one's orientation to the world".

One case study in which the oceanic feeling could serve as a doorway to a deeper understanding of our unconscious desires is Marine Girls, true heroines of lo-fi pop. Marine Girls recorded songs of radical cuteness and unbound love and are probably one of the best examples of applied marine unconsciousness as an escape from the patriarchal modes of desire.

Marine Girls were a shooting star in the indie scene; they burned out rather quickly. They started recording music in 1980 and they broke up in 1983. The group was formed by four girls: Tracey Thorn, Gina Hartman and the Fox sisters, Alice and Jane. They recorded one extremely DIY tape called *A Day by the Sea* and an album, *Beach Party*, both rough and sweet lo-fi gems. They disbanded as soon as they got into university. The split was all but pleasant, a real teenage affair:

Our split was perhaps the most rock 'n' roll thing we ever did, in that in took place in a dressing room, after a fraught gig at which we were heckled, and was not without acrimony. We were very young, so the aftermath was poorly handled by all of us, and it was years before we ever talked to each other about it, and made our peace with the mess we'd made.

Alice and Jane Fox ended up in Brighton, while Tracey Thorn moved to Hull. They still released another album, *Lazy Ways.* It's a little more polished, less lo-fi. Less magical, overall — at least as far as I'm concerned. Their run as a group is not drenched in the rock 'n' roll extremisms of someone like Brian Wilson and it was not a life-consuming calling as it was for R. Stevie Moore and Daniel Johnston. Their story is quite unadorned and not very rockstar-esque at all. It's more like a rush of teenage love or a riot, rather than a rock band hagiography — it faded fast and, where it does linger, it does so like a bruise.

Their untimely demise notwithstanding, it's hard to imagine a more crucial band for a book such as this. Aside from being possibly one of the greatest indie miracles of the 1980s, within the history of lo-fi Marine Girls insist on the scene as an unanswered question: What about gender? Up until this point, after all, lo-fi looked pretty much like a boys' club. The desires that riddled the previous pages were admittedly very masculine, for a lack of more cutting words. Brian Wilson's neuroses, dreaming his high-school ex and all; R. Stevie Moore's aggressive will to be the best of all; Daniel Johnston's borderline creepy obsession with Laurie — there might be something universal in these sorts of yearning, but they are all, also, heavily gendered experiences. They were boys, socialized as boys, experiencing loss, lust, despair as boys. Their gendered position in our contemporary society certainly was a ghostly presence in all their hustling and bustling against this world. And in their music too, of course. Gender was a large question mark waiting to pop.

Marine Girls, on the contrary, were militantly feminine in everything they did. The desires that animated their songs were always spoken of from a feminine perspective. And not just because they were, so to speak, biologically an all-girl group, mind you. The expression of their gendered position was purposeful, at times even exaggerated for seemingly tactical reasons. They wanted to sing about what they felt in the most uncompromising way possible. They were well aware that they were living in a patriarchal society and they wanted to use lo-fi music and its DIY ethos to fully express the Otherness that patriarchy constructs for itself, pushing the possibility of femininity to its most extreme, dazzling excesses. They sung about boys unabashedly, in a manner that was sometimes even off-putting in its unending adorableness and awkwardness. Spliced in, constant, evocative references to the sea: a formless mass to get lost by, a mirror of such a radical delicateness:

> We used to get up on stage in front of mostly male crowds who'd come to see a rock gig, and we'd quietly but defiantly play our heartfelt songs about boys we loved or boys we despised, mixing in strange and ever-so-slightly random references to the sea.

They wanted to be atrociously tender, devastatingly cute. Not because women are biologically like that, but to reclaim their own desires to the fullest, embodying maleness's absolute Outside. Marine Girls practiced Hélène Cixous's ethical injunction and understood its power:

> Woman must write her self: must write about women and bring women to writing, from which they have been driven away as violently as from their bodies — for the same reasons, by the same law, with the same fatal goal [...] But first it must be said that in spite of the enormity of the repression that has kept them in the "dark" — that dark which people have been trying to make them accept as their attribute — there is, at this time, no general woman, no one typical woman. What they have in common I will say. But what strikes me is the infinite richness of their individual constitutions: you can't talk about a female sexuality, uniform, homogeneous, classifiable into codes — any more than you can talk about one unconscious resembling another. Women's imaginary is inexhaustible, like music, painting, writing: their stream of phantasms is incredible.

If patriarchal capitalism made them girls, they would bite back by becoming the most unmanageable version of femininity ever conceived. Cuteness and love so strong you're bound to lose yourself.

Their music has often been categorized as post-punk. It's an ill-fitting category, honestly. Their music is way out there, even for post-punk standards, but, historically speaking, it makes sense. As they emerged onto the indie scene, other bands, all loosely rising from the ashes of punk rock and all playing some shade of rough guitar music, were experimenting with exuberant non-maleness. Two of the most prominent examples were the Raincoats and the Slits, two acts often mentioned in the same breath as Marine Girls, despite their respective irreducible uniqueness.

The Slits played a nervous strain of disfigured rock 'n' roll, bastardized with dance and reggae echoes. They sounded extremely tough, an all-out feminist aggression. Their 1979 record *Cut* was characterized by aggressive, nervous grooves: the grotesquely dark staccato of "Typical Girls" and "Shoplifting" or the sunshine discordance of "Adventures Close to Home" and "So Tough" — real odes to girls *payin' fuck all* to the laws patriarchy had set in place for them. The girls stood on the cover naked from the waist upwards, a declaration of war rather than an album cover. The Raincoats, on the other hand, were just as combative, albeit in a weirder sense. They played deconstructed jingle jangles with razor-thin guitars and voices flying all over the place. They were less tough than the Slits, at least on the face of it, and a little more convoluted, so to speak. The crowning jewel of their self-titled 1979 record was a cover of the Kinks' "Lola". The song told the story of a man encountering a trans woman and depicts the transphobic horror that grips the straight guy upon realising his partner's gender. The Raincoats took the track and genderfucked it, flipping the original's transphobia on its head. They did not swap the gender of the protagonist; the two singers, Ana de Silva and Gina Birch, sang it from the male perspective. Were the protagonists of the story both trans now? Did it even matter? The message was nonetheless quite deliberate and clear: fuck off.

Still, even among such peers, Marine Girls' feminist poetics stood as a unique creature — a far more radical and weirder one. They did not look menacing at all. On the contrary, they appeared as heralds of utmost delicacy. They were kawaii, the epitome of un-bellicose. They were unsettling, disquieting in subtler ways. In a voluntarily, excessively soft way, actually. They talked about love, love, love — and the sea, which, in their songs, was love incarnate. They were also fairly straight, but again in a deliberate, subversive way, so to speak: boys were never the subject, always the object. Whether loved or despised, the male gaze and its demands were pushed to the outer limits of their scenes. It was never the focal point. Heterosexuality turned on its head. They sang as if society was already not male-dominated. As if the act of singing as a woman about women's feelings was already an end to patriarchal control in some decisive sense. While the Slits and the Raincoats fought against male subjection, Marine Girls uncannily went about their art as if they had already won and they were free to strut about innocent and untouched. They behaved like successful escapees out of the patriarchal world, with their tender heart on show for all to see.

Another thing that set them aside from their post-punk peers were their main musical influences. Again, there was something oddly gentle about the influences they wore on their sleeves. While the rest of the post-punks were clearly indebted to punk and its legacy, alongside other more or less experimental genres, Marine Girls were fond of much gentler, untimely music: Sixties girl-groups and sunshine pop. They found inspiration in the Ronettes, the Shirelles and the Shangri-Las, rather than the cock-rock-by-other-means of the Sex Pistols or the Clash. Their sound was inspired by an incredibly uncool sort of pop, especially at the cusp of the hyper-modern Eighties. They were fans of the least aggressive pop of them all, the opposite of most of their peers. Their songs were full of backing choirs responding to the main vocal line. The melodies were snappy and pure fun, recalling that innocent joy that makes sunshine pop so endearing. They imitated the girl-groups' uncanny sweetness and their harmonies, mudding them in amateur musicianship and starkly lo-fi recordings. Not as an act of vandalism, mind you, but as a profound form of reckless, amateurish admiration. Again, out of sheer love.

The further thing that set them apart from the other post-punk bands was precisely their unflinching practice of lo-fi recording. Sure, the Slits' and the Raincoats' records were rough, but it's hard to express just how radical Marine Girls' commitment to DIY recording actually was. Saying that their scant output sounded extremely lo-fi would be selling short their sonic poverty. Their albums, especially their masterpiece *Beach Party*, give off the vibe of something being played by a kitchen sink or in a living room — they sound really, really "bad". And the sonic poverty did not stop at the recording quality, either. Even the instruments they played and how they played them displayed an absolute commitment to a no-tech hard-line. The percussion consisted of simple wooden boxes, the guitars are strummed quite primitively. The chord progressions are shockingly simple: no extra note is ever present. The voices sometimes shake or hum along the melodies quite loosely. The songs were breezy and dreamy, but also extremely barren, abrupt, very short. The tunes hardly exceeded the two-minute mark or so. Marine Girls' songs were minimal, undemanding, skeletal. They sounded like a pop group stripped to its bones. They begged the question of just how lo-fi you could go: can you strip this song down even further? Is this chord too much? Could you do even less or way worse? They opened new horizons of sonic sabotage. They did not only refuse the studio-form, like the other artists we have met thus far; they downright impoverished the sounds of pop itself to the extreme. A sort of sonic subtractive absolutism, if you will.

All of this would surely be enough to consider them quite a remarkable band, and an essential entry in our tentative lo-fi canon. Their unique softness and their sonic poverty would certainly make them worthy of all our consideration. Nonetheless, this also constitutes the surface of Marine Girls' disruptiveness. It's the tip of the iceberg, really. The depth of the feminine uncanny they militantly embodied would still be untouched, unexplored. That oceanic feeling they uniquely unearthed absolutely outshines every other feature of their music. It's not an exaggeration to say that there is something unspeakable in their lyrics and in the way they sang them. Something quite magical, clearly unique. And the only way to properly convey just how dazzling it actually is is to zoom in on their most accomplished record, *Beach Party*.

The album starts with "In Love". Kurt Cobain, a fan of the band, thought that this was the archetypical Marine Girls song and it's really hard to disagree with him. Once, Courtney Love even told Tracey Thorn that Kurt meant to cover it at some point. Thorn met Love on *Later with Jools Holland*, where she was to perform with Massive Attack: "'y'know, Kurt always wanted to do a cover of that song of yours, "In Love".' More or less speechless, I managed to mumble something polite in return, before she strode back and the show continued", she would later recall. "In Love" is essentially a pop tune, albeit with a couple of jaw-dropping quirks going on for it.

Musically speaking, it's very much like a flat surface, never changing but irradiating a sense of restless movement. It's monotonous, circling back around the same melodies and chords, but it's never tedious. On the contrary, it is extremely energetic, be it for the various singers' broken voices or the tentative, shaky strumming that infuses the track with a sense that it is about to fall apart at any moment. The lyrics are barebone: it's about an ex who found a new lover. The protagonist looks at her former partner's new life and repeats, without shouting or commotion but certainly with a fair amount of bad blood, *I hear you're in love*. The rest of the track is solely dedicated to the recriminations of the protagonist: glad to hear you're feeling better, that you found another and all that jazz. On the face of it, it's a rather simple post-break-up song. But there's an intensity to it, which turns this familiar scenario into something absolute, totalizing.

First of all, it is sung in a first-person perspective so narrow it almost sucks the air out of the world. Everything is eclipsed in this girl's sentimental abandon. There's nothing but this girl's heartbreak in all its teenage intensity. She is a living black hole. The only intrusion is a quaint *la-la-la-la* repeating in the background and the extremely minimal, repetitive instrumental backing it all up; an intrusion that, in its minuscule proportions, only exasperates the enormity of the feeling. It is veritably the sounds of a feeling so bad it melts the subject experiencing it.

Secondly, the object of her love, clearly male, is at the outskirts of the scene, neither relevant nor interesting. His agency in all of this is inconsequential. There's just her, dissolved in the pure expression of her wounded love. The track lacks any sort of male perspective, and purposefully so. At the heart of it all, it's not the treachery that's important, but the ravenous, destituting process that is happening through this girl and this girl alone. The crux of it all is the sentiment itself, which undoes the normal life of the person undergoing it — something that Deleuze and Guattari defined as a "becoming-woman".

A becoming-woman, of course, does not mean, for Deleuze and Guattari, literally becoming a woman — even though, as we've seen, Marine Girls did not shy away from singing from a gendered perspective at all. On the contrary, a becoming-woman could affect "all of humankind, men and women both". It could happen to you, me or anyone, really. It is an intense process of ravishing that tears apart property, ownership and control. "They create only by making possible a becoming over which they do not have ownership, into which they themselves must enter". Rather than being the unfolding of some biological destiny that would lead some people straight to womanhood, it is a movement that happens to all of those who fall out, above or below the control of the majoritarian, male normality. It is an unnatural and militant kind of femininity, then, a "minoritarian, sorcerous one too", as Deleuze and Guattari would have it: "becoming-woman, more than any other becoming, possesses a special introductory power; it is not so much that women are witches, but that sorcery proceeds by way of this becoming-woman". It's the same kind of femininity deployed by Marine Girls to put their desire on the record fully, unabashedly, at its fullest intensity. They did not sing as girls following the compulsion of some hidden biological or theological design, but to gain a space outside male domination. Or as Deleuze and Guattari would have it:

Use love and consciousness to abolish subjectification: "To become the great lover, the magnetizer and catalyzer … one has to first experience the profound wisdom of being an utter fool." Use the *I* think for a becoming-animal, and love for a becoming-woman of man. Desubjectify consciousness and passion.

Circling back to "In Love" and putting it in simpler words, the heart of the song is a becoming-woman because the song is this and only this: *a girl, ravished and undone.*

This scene serves as a blueprint for the entire Marine Girls' discography: most of it is an airing out of feminine ravishment, of a becoming-woman in a world where such an enjoyment is usually barred, repressed or belittled. Most of their songs, possibly all of them, are a direct expression of being taken by those feelings that society deems silly, childish, foolish or girly and getting lost in them, experiencing their immensity to the point of having to revert to a language and sound so simple it mimics the child-like aphasia love forces us to sink into. Their sound imitates and induces that feeling of being fully possessed by something otherworldly, unshakeable, completely out of our social and individual control — or, in other words, ego-loss in the face of love. Or, again, real enjoyment itself, without restrictions or boundaries. "It is urgent to defend love's subversive, heterogeneous relationship to the law [...] The identity cult of repetition must be challenged by love of what is different, is unique, is unrepeatable, unstable and foreign", once wrote the French philosopher Alain Badiou, and Marine Girls went most definitely out of their way to involuntarily heed his call.

The first half of the album follows the schema almost to a tee. "Fridays, Tonight" and "Times We Used to Spend" are both songs about heartbreak in all its tireless intensity. They're all extremely simple tracks, almost to the point of being musically evanescent. The point of the songs is always the same, unchanging: a great process of ravishment, a sentimentality forced to the brink — almost to the point of sounding absurd in its teenage sincerity, or exaggerated in its absoluteness. There's an undefeated intensity in the simplicity and undying momentum as they sing:

> *I know you never loved*
> *Why did you say you cared*

Or when they mouth spitefully melancholic lines like:

> *When I hear that tune on the record player*
> *When I hear that song on the breeze*
> *Thinking of the times we used to spend together.*

A movement outwards pushed by the dispossessing throes of love.

With "Honey", the first half of the record peaks. It's a perfect pop song drenched in echoing low production, like "In Love" and others that will soon follow — catchy to the point of prompting a million re-listens at first impact. The circling chord progression is rudimentary, to say the least: D to an E to a G to an A then back to a D. Thematically, the song explodes Marine Girls' becoming-woman, taking its two main characteristics to the extreme: the undoing, ravishing process and the complete side-stepping of any male perspective.

The song is not about heartbreak this time around, but is of course a love song of some sort nonetheless. A girl has treated a boy wrong, even though she loves him still. He doesn't understand the situation, but the whole thing is happening in and to the girl — and the girl only — regardless. He may desire to control her somehow, but every attempt is futile:

> *Honey wants possession of my heart*
> *Wants to know the secret of my dreams*
> *Doesn't understand my treachery.*

Then the girl erupts in a confession of unbridled passion and pure indifference to the boy's perspective:

> *I know I'll love him forever or until I find another boy.*

The feeling is absolute, boundless. There's nothing but the girl following the flux of her desires, which in its most unbridled form is a love that could last forever, impossibly demanding and growing in her chest like wilderness. An object-less love, though, since the boy could easily be replaced without losing this momentum. A pure becoming led only by intensity — motivated only by the need to be more than what this world permits us to be. Nothing could contain her escape from every restriction. It's a sabotage of all heterosexual expectation or norm regarding a girl's innermost wants and needs — femininity completely unbound from any male perspective or justification. Again, a textbook case of becoming-woman, at least according to Deleuze and Guattari:

> *Honey knows I never lie and I'll be his until this*
> *feeling dies.*

Past this point, the beach mysteriously beckons In fact, after "Honey", the sea begins to appear as the protagonist of most of the songs, insistently. The oceanic feeling hits us unprompted, right after this intense declaration of open desire. And its appearance is almost kitsch: seagulls and waves, the first sounds opening "Holiday Song". The sea sounds are probably the first (and last) thing that could be described as lush, or something to that effect, on the album. Or, at least, they could be described as not being minimal to the point of being about to crumble into a million bits — especially compared to the elementary chord progression and tin-can percussion that accompany them. The lyrics are, again, about the psychedelia of getting lost in love. And again, the lyrics are so basic in the words they use and the rhyme scheme they deploy that they perfectly and performatively convey the wordlessness that hits you when you fall in love with someone. It's as if they weren't words at all:

> *Bring me the moon, we can play on the sand*
> *Give me a smile, I will give you my hand*
> *Take off your shoes and we'll run to the sea*
> *As soon as dawn, you can come home with me.*

The ocean appears as the symbol of losing the grip on everything. A psychic stand-in for infatuated ego-loss, as it was for Theweleit's Nazis, but this time around with an overwhelmingly positive connotation: it's the gateway to the great psychic outdoors beyond this world.

If, for Theweleit's ultra-male Nazis, the psychic sea and its oceanic feeling loomed as a nightmarish feminine invasion, here it dawns on the protagonist as the sort of totalizing satisfaction she always dreamed off — the absolute love that unbinds you from yourself and all drudgery. The sea is, for Marine Girls, that very becoming-woman that ravishes and transfigures. But, this time, by the sea, it is finally free to run amok, unencumbered by dull boys and the sad heartbreaks they cause and their unappealing mundanity. Or, if you're feeling maximalist, the sea is that which "escapes the flux of the realisation of the world", as the anti-philosopher and sailor Gilles Grelet would put it. The sea appears as an escape from any sort of scarcity or enclosure or male domination or heartbreak. It's just love, love, love intensely — to the point of breaking down to its most basic elements:

> *Steal me a lighthouse that shines so clear*
> *We'll look at the stars as we lie on the pier*
> *When the sun rises I'll be here with you*
> *Down on the beach until the summer's through*

The subsequent songs make this idea pleonastic: as soon as the sea pops up in a song, we find ourselves lost in foolish love — outside the bounds of constricting coercions and compulsive male-centredness. When it appears, an alien femininity seeps through the cracks of Marine Girls' pop songs as this vast unfolding of unconstrained energies. The feeling might usually veer to the negative side of things, as was the case for the heartbreak in their early songs, but it's always suspended in this amniotic sack of bliss: the longing and melancholy exuding on songs like "Day-Night Dreams" or "Promises" is punctured by the squawking of seagulls or the constant references to long weekends out of town by an iridescent beach or water-y things, as if they were incarnations of a desire that stops everything around it and undoes the habitual flow of earthly things:

> *There she sits without a thought in her head*
> *Unfinished letters on an unmade bed*
> *Losing count of her many lovers*
> *Paints her life in watercolours.*

The Situationists, a French insurrectionary art group, often used the slogan "Beneath the concrete, the beach". It was a call to arms to spur people onwards towards the wonders that could come from a more or less violent interruption of everyday life. Their theory was that existence under capitalism could go on only through a constant containment (the concrete) of humanity's actual needs and desires (the beach). As Guy Debord, one of the fundamental figures of the Situationist movement, put it:

> The use of everyday life, in the sense of a consumption of lived time, is governed by the reign of scarcity: scarcity of free time and scarcity of possible uses of this free time. Just as the accelerated history of our time is the history of accumulation and industrialization, so the backwardness and conservative tendencies of everyday life are products of the laws and interests that have presided over this industrialization.

But beneath the suffocation of modern, alienated life still lies a fuller existence: that repressed promise Marcuse talked about. It's not like capitalism could completely snuff out our unconscious drives, right? Through a total re-appropriation of our desires, especially in their most quotidian, banal aspects, we could still overcome our capitalist libidinal drought, at least according to Debord:

> Capitalist civilization has not yet been superseded anywhere, but it continues to produce its own enemies everywhere. This next attempt at a total contestation of capitalism will know how to invent and propose a different use of everyday life, and will immediately base itself on new everyday practices and on new types of human relationships.

Marine Girls, with their violent oceanic cuteness and unmanned becoming-woman, were surely digging for the treasures underneath our grey existence, reappropriating the rupturing strength of the lovely and the girly. Their oceanic feeling, with its totalizing intensity, was, willingly or not, an experiment in a new type of human relationality outside of capitalist and patriarchal norms, expressed in music.

This oceanic rupture mounts throughout the record, with songs like the eponymous "Marine Girls" and "The Lure of the Rockpools", until it reaches its apex in one of the last songs on the album, "20,000 Leagues". It's a disquieting piece of pure, even fatal desire taking place in the bowels of the ocean. The story it tells is quite surreal — a girl is given a rendezvous at the bottom of the sea:

> *20,000 leagues under the sea*
> *That's where my baby said he'd meet me*

20,000 leagues under the sea
That's where he said I'd have to be

The boy, as usual, is not there, and even if he were, would she care? The libidinal descent into the depths of the ocean, the only relevant thing about this encounter, spells out the death of the girl's subjectivity, or something to that effect. As the song progresses, the girl melts away and the movement that brings her deep to the heart of darkness takes centre stage. The scene gets more and more grotesque and, all around her, everything dissipates:

20,000 leagues down, down, down
20,000 leagues down from town
20,000 league's worth of breath
20,000 leagues, near to death

The deeper she goes, the more she's ripped open by her desire. She's out of breath, out of reach, out of bounds. Even the environment surrounding her simply fades out of view, becoming an integral part of this oceanic becoming-woman:

20,000 leagues, will you be there?
20,000 leagues, I didn't swear
20,000 leagues, where seaweed is red
20,000 leagues, where starfish are dead

Love at its fullest. Every fixed habit melts out of her, in this ultimate escape from everything there is. This song exemplifies the unspeakable that lies within Marine Girls. This terroristic femininity, an absolute embrace of the outside.

The Marine Girls faded fast, we know it by now, but their legacy lingered. Tracey Thorn collaborated with Massive Attack and founded Everything But The Girl. With their raw display of sweetness and unmusicianship, they inspired the sound of a very cute-committed strain of lo-fi music, often called twee — Tallulah Gosh and all the bands gravitating around Sarah Records or Beat Happening, the band who brought Marine Girls' records to America, and all the bands around K Records or, again, more recent indie darlings like Veronica Falls or the Pains of Being Pure at Heart. Distant echoes of their ethos of reckless love could even be heard, amidst her many Elliott Smith allusions, in the music of someone like Phoebe Bridgers, especially in her lyrics — so militantly committed to speaking from a gendered position and thoroughly possessed by the amazement of being "always surprised by what I do for love".

This summer, the sci-fi writer Charlie Jane Anders penned an interesting manifesto for a movement she calls "sweetweird". According to her: "a spectre is haunting pop culture — an adorable and friendly, but slightly messed-up creature that beckons us into a world of kindness and surrealism". This spectre is sweetweird, a loose canon of cultural products that blend the lovely and the uncanny in a conscious effort to break the mould of normality:

> The core idea of sweetweird is: the world makes no sense, but we can be nurturing, frivolous and kind. We don't have to respond to the ludicrous illogic of the world around us by turning mean and nasty, or by expecting everyone else to be horrible. At the very least, we can carve out

friendly, supportive spaces in the midst of chaotic nonsense, and maybe help each other survive.

Rather than accepting a miserable existence in a hard world, sweetweird proposes an escape through kind oddities and lovely strangeness. "Wherever surrealism and kindness join in a beautifully unholy union, there you will find sweetweird." It's hard not to read Marine Girls' becoming-woman — disquieting, lovely, militant — and their embrace of their surreal, oceanic femininity as sweetweird *ante litteram*. Really, how else could you describe them other than sweet and weird? Rather than playing by the boys' rules, they chose a much stranger path, leading lo-fi to places it had never been before:

> Let's embrace preposterousness, and each other. We can build ridiculous worlds and fill them with generosity. Things are going to be extremely weird no matter what we do — but we have the power to make them sweet, as well.

Marine Girls certainly tried, sitting by their psychic ocean.

World class contrarian

Ariel Pink and the ideology of contrarianism

The sterile and pathological solitude of the Ego does not deserve the
name of life, just as the treasure of the miser is not wealth,
not even personal wealth
Amadeo Bordiga

"MUSICIAN UNFAIRLY CANCELLED AFTER
CAPITAL HILL RIOT", reads the Fox News banner right
under Tucker Carlson's chest. "You're an artist. Artists do
transgressive things and you did the most transgressive thing:
you came out as a public Trump supporter and then you
went to a Trump rally", says the infamous pundit looking
at someone right in front of him, just outside the camera's
frame. "What happened next?"

The camera cuts to Ariel Pink sitting like a child in detention
— shoulders slouched forward, droopy eyes, head rocking
back and forth in small circles. He's squeezing the most pitiful
expression out of his face. He looks like he's on the verge of
tears. A Star of David hangs from his neck between the heart-
dotted collar of his buttoned-up shirt. "I went to the White
House… to see our President…" Pink confesses, "went to the
hotel, took a nap… End of story… I was there for a peaceful
rally."

The rally Ariel Pink is talking about happened to run parallel to the storming of Capitol Hill, on January 6th 2021. That day is burned in my memory as one of the most bizarre events in American and global history. A masterclass in involuntary surrealism and collective despair. The mob that attacked Capitol Hill had one simple goal: enact a coup in the heart of the West. They wanted to stop the election of Joe Biden and overturn Donald Trump's electoral failure. They were all convinced that the election was fake or at least somewhat fraudulent, or something along those lines. Trump was the rightful president; they had to take the power back — not to keep it for themselves or the people at large, God forbid, but give it back to him straight away.

Of course, the plan did not go through. The images and news broadcasted to the world in those frantic hours were shocking in their farcical irreality. Rioters in paramilitary gear were storming Statuary Hall, rigorously respecting the red cordons that keep people away from the statues like tourists would. People were, apparently, dying from being tased on their ball sacks by the police, who were otherwise outnumbered inside the White House corridors. A half-naked man with a shamanic headdress on his head was flexing his muscles where the president of the United States usually sits. Despite the obvious reality of the violence — five people lost their lives during the event, after all — for twenty-four hours it felt like a *Family Guy* episode with potentially enormous geopolitical implications. The sense that this thing was too outside the realm of the plausible to be actually unfolding in front of our screens was palpable. Ariel Pink was actually not there. He was no insurrectionist, he claims again and again. But he was close enough, physically and ideologically, to cause an upheaval in the indie scene.

The news of his presence in Washington came from a post on Alex Lee Moyer's Instagram account. Moyer is a documentarian. Her first movie, *TFW No GF*, was solely dedicated to incel culture and was scored by Ariel Pink himself. Her second, *Alex's War*, focused on Alex Jones, the conspiracy theorist and ideologue of the Capitol Hill rioters. Her Instagram post depicted Ariel Pink and fellow lo-fi wunderkind John Maus in D.C., right when the riot was taking place. Soon, Pink took to Twitter to confirm that his presence there was unrelated, but no mistake:

> i was in dc to peacefully show my support for the president. i attended the rally on the white house lawn and went back to hotel and took a nap. case closed.

Be it a peaceful protest or narcolepsy, his label, Mexican Summer, dropped him soon after nonetheless. To recover from the event, Pink did what any artist in the twenty-first century would do to cope with the aftermath of potentially world-historical events: he dropped a series of NFTs.

What a weird twist in lo-fi history.

After all, Ariel Pink has always been one of the most refined and appreciated contemporary lo-fi artists. And with good reason, too. It's hard to name a better songwriter and musician in the entire lo-fi canon, and outside of it as well. His many albums are sophisticated blends of artful sonic poverty and an unparalleled knack for pop music. His songs are catchy and, sonically speaking, deliriously witty and surprising. The music critic Simon Reynolds at one point claimed that Ariel Pink was his "favourite musician of the 2000s", and it's really hard to disagree with him. He has been one of the crowning jewels of lo-fi's rise to *Pitchfork* fame in the 2010s.

Ariel Pink has truly been, within and without lo-fi, a watershed musician in many senses. He is an elegant stylist of poor sounds. But he is also an artist that deserves vigilant scrutiny, especially after his nap in Washington. He has not only been an outstanding artist, but also — and possibly more importantly at this point — the aesthetic embodiment of a malaise and a distaste for this world we ought to reckon with if we truly want to ponder on lo-fi as an escape from our capitalist present. It would be facile and uninformative — and possibly politically unhelpful — to just dismiss him on the grounds of being a Trump supporter, surely, but we must also reflect upon what sort of zeitgeist is condensed in such an act and in such an artist. We must ask ourselves what he and his art say about lo-fi's longing for a way out.

We must ask these questions even more pressingly when we realize that Ariel Pink's D.C. escapade was hardly the first questionable thing he has ever done in the public eye. He is an artist whose ethos and poetics have proven to be, time and again, quite controversial, even before he came out as a proper Trump truther. He has said and done things that could be considered, from a radical perspective, worthy of critique, at the very least. He has occupied his place in indie stardom as a prankster, a disrupter, as a sick kid fighting against everything all the time — sometimes with dubious results. His Twitter handle is "World Class Contrarian", after all.

One time he said that it's not illegal to be racist; another, that gay marriage pisses him off; and on one occasion he even said that he loves necrophiliacs. Does he believe any of these things? That's beside the point. But my favourite applied example of his contrarianism is the beef he had with Madonna and Grimes somewhen in 2014. Readers be warned: we're entering the realm of gossip. The gist of the story is this: Ariel Pink claimed he was asked to write some music for Madonna's new album. He then said that he despised everything Madonna had ever done past her first album. Her career has been, according to him, a "downward slide" — which is honestly ridiculous in a timeline where *True Blue* exists. Grimes then chimed in accusing him of "delusional misogyny", since Pink said that Madonna's producers needed her to "come up with a new techno jam for her to gyrate to and pretend that she's 20 years old" — an ageist comment you don't often hear levied against, say, Steve Tyler fumbling on stage. "Also ray of light is a masterpiece", Grimes tweeted that faithful October — and she is honestly not wrong at all. In response, Pink called Grimes "stupid and retarded". He then cried over his cancellation, or whatever you want to call the obvious backlash.

In both of Pink's comments — indeed, in all of his inflammatory remarks — there's a feature that makes them the glaring work of a contrarian: the comments are not meant for the direct victim, but are directed at the shared morality of the spectatorship at large. Both the idea that Madonna's music sucks and the word "retarded" are aimed at the people somewhere off in the distance, who will take offence, not Pink's interlocutor. The moral value attacked changes in the two comments — Madonna's pop music is good; you shouldn't say slurs — but the intention remains the same: deface the shared morality of the Big Other watching at home (The People, The Crowd, The Feminists, The Media, etc., etc.). When looked at correctly, even the Capitol Hill incident was like this: he was there, not for the riot or to enforce violent change, but to make a spectacle out of his provocation. It was all a matter of creating an image for an external audience. What's the endgame? Not a revolution, nor a reform of our moral values — something which could be judged for its necessity or desirability. On the contrary, it's simply about being scolded. These sorts of comments do not propose any sort of adjustment in our moral compass, but they paradoxically seek to reinforce it by forcing outrage and disdain out of people. This sort of contrarianism is actually a quest for a scolder — an executioner, even. That is, until the public's attention bleeds dry and a new provocation has to be done, of course. It feels — and it is — like endlessly running in a circle. And, as we shall see, running in a circle is, in a sense, the disquieting grandeur of Ariel Pink poetics, his calling card.

I say "disquieting" because I tend to agree with Pink's fellow sleepyhead John Maus. When this story broke, Maus went to Pink's rescue with a now-deleted Twitter thread. In it, Maus said that Pink should not be judged with the same metric we'd use with "normal" citizens, since he is the messenger of a phantasmatic crowd living outside the realm of normality. His music is an escape from our shared reality and its values, and his opinions, of course, mirror that same exteriority:

> To claim that Ariel "hates women" is false because it neglects a greater and more important truth: what he affirms and defends in everything, precisely, are the innumerable queers that the residues of a sexual economy ordered to the sanctioned identities of "man" and "women" only ever violently arrest […] Ariel Pink is not a misogynist. He is a nymphomaniac, a little girl, a dog, etc.

This is most certainly correct: Pink speaks for and like an evanescent people that fell out of consensus reality and nurtured a real hatred for the world aboveground. In this, Ariel Pink is, at the end of the day, not dissimilar from the lo-fi pioneers we have met thus far. But Maus's platitudes are disingenuous and his exonerations misplaced at best, if not downright fraudulent. Pink speaks for a certain strain of weirdos, a specific kind of outsiders. Which *sort of outsideness*, though, especially in light of his political allegiances, remains to be clarified. His values and his escape from this world should be probed further still.

Ariel Pink's career began when the folkadelic superstars Animal Collective found a CD-R of his in their tour van. The demo was called *Worn Copy*, one of the countless tapes Pink had recorded since the late 1990s. The legend goes that, as soon as they played it, they fell in love with the strange pop coming out of their stereos. At the time, Animal Collective had just kickstarted their own record label, Paw Tracks. Up until that point, they had just released Animal Collective-related stuff, but Pink would soon become their first exception. They wanted to re-release *Worn Copy*, but Ariel Pink refused. Instead, he asked them to re-issue the record that still stands to this day as his most accomplished work, *The Doldrums*. He had recorded *The Doldrums* during a brutal drug binge and, compared to *Worn Copy*, it was a much darker project. The song that gives the album its name, for example, opens with the chilling lines:

> *I'm living with myself today*
> *With barely anything to say*
> *I'm living with my problems and*
> *Can't do a thing about them*

He recorded the whole thing with a three-stringed guitar. Animal Collective were not immediately enamoured with such a hostile project, but they eventually agreed to re-release it.

Ariel Pink started playing music at an early age, when he was just a teenager:

> When I was in high school, at my dad's house, I had a garage that I called the Lab. I just had a bass guitar, some kitchen utensils — cheese graters and stuff like that. I had one amp. I used to record on a handheld, miniature cassette recorder — a voice recorder with a little tape in it.

Back then, his output mostly comprised of John Cage-ish and krautrock-inspired experimental pieces. It was only in 1997 when he decided to christen his experiments as Ariel Pink's Haunted Graffiti, the moniker that would accompany his one-man project for most of his life.

That moniker, a name he'd eventually shed only in 2022 to take up the way kookier Ariel Pink's Dark Side, and the relationship he had with it shine an interesting light on Pink as an artist and the sort of lo-fi he was inspired by. Whenever someone would refer to him as "Ariel Pink" — a name, be it real or fictional, detached from the glamorous irreality of his one-man band — he'd get iffy:

> It's not a persona. My name is not Ariel Pink, it's Ariel Rosenberg. In the early days, it was a home recording project and it was called Ariel Pink's Haunted Graffiti. I wasn't Ariel Pink — that was the name of the thing. This somehow was too

hard for promoters to remember and for people
to think about.

Just like Ziggy Stardust, Ariel Pink was a sort of imaginary
creature, untethered from Ariel Rosenberg's real existence,
created to funnel the music and the vision of the Haunted
Graffitis. Most people, me included, would go on to consider
Ariel Pink the most proper way to address his output, since
he never really switched it up in any relevant way, but he
always treated it as something which could be discarded: an
imaginary character, not a persona, built to be larger-than-
life and out of this world; a maquillage to cover his actual
existence as a human and elevate his art to the world of
superstardom. He was a loner self-producing all of his music
on his own; he has never spent a consistent amount of time
in an actual. He has done very little to make something that
could have been played on some mainstream radio, sure, but
he nonetheless wanted to use the grammar and the glamour
that the stars had been using throughout pop history. Just like
R. Steve Moore, he is an outsider glam rocker.

In fact, Ariel Pink took R. Stevie Moore as a model to style
his art after as soon as he heard his music. Their aspirations
and goals became basically identical from the moment Pink
laid his hands on a collection of R. Stevie Moore's tracks: they
both wanted to be rockstars, ditching any of the conventional
mores to get there. Pink had surely found a kindred spirit.
"I'd heard one album a couple of years before I recorded *The
Doldrums* called *Everything You Ever Wanted to Know about R. Stevie
Moore but Were Too Afraid to Ask*. After that, I was hooked."
Ariel Pink, just like R. Stevie Moore, behaved like a rockstar
without ever being one in the proper sense of the word.

After his encounter with R. Stevie Moore's music, Pink not only took up and continued Moore's rock 'n' roll ambitions, he also fashioned his sounds after him. Or, better, he started quoting his mannerisms, oddities and idiosyncrasies with surgical precision. But it was not a rip-off, really. It was something more refined: a study of sorts, of a very peculiar way to go about pop music. He deconstructed his style, highlighting that peak of oddity or perfecting that other vocal inflection or tape-hissed chord progression. He took R. Stevie Moore's way of doing pop music and he inscribed his own signature genius upon it. Nowhere is this clearer than on *The Doldrums*. Sometimes, while listening to that album, something will come along that will immediately sound like a sample of an R. Stevie Moore song; the perfect replica of Moore's unique craft. Take, for example, the valiumed-up glam swagger of "Among Dreams" or the epic T-Rex-isms of "Grey Sunset" — they've got R. Stevie Moore written all over them.

And of course, it's not a surprise to discover that Pink recorded *The Doldrums* right after discovering that very R. Stevie Moore compilation. He sent the album to his newfound idol immediately after completing the tape. R. Stevie Moore wrote an email back to him completely blown away. He was so amazed by this young disciple that he wanted to collaborate straight away. Apparently, it was also the first email Ariel Pink got on his Hotmail account:

> So I sent him a surprise burned CD of *The Doldrums*, which I'd just finished, and an introductory note and a request for some cassette titles from his canon. He promptly replied in an email (my first EVER email, in fact, having just opened my first ever Hotmail account!)

> and to my utter shock and star-struck glee, he
> was blown away by *The Doldrums* and instantly
> offered if I'd like to collaborate! I was absolutely
> beside myself, and humbled beyond words.

R. Stevie Moore was not the only one to receive this sort of treatment. On the contrary, but again taking after R. Stevie Moore's scatter-brained eclecticism, it is quite plain to see that most of Ariel Pink's music is a series of indirect and erudite quotes from the most disparate sources, all arching backwards towards pop's past glories. On *The Doldrums*, one could easily argue that there's a fair amount of the Cure — in the suspended synth and dramatic lyrics in "Envelopes Another Day" that, for example, recall the fading image of both "Plainsong" and "All Cats Are Grey". And throughout his career, one could lose oneself counting all the instances he has used materials from his musical memory to construct his pop Frankensteinian monsters. His albums are constant throwbacks to anything from the cheesiest glam rock of bands like Def Leppard and Mötley Crüe to the most sombre of darkwave and the most obnoxious bubble-gum pop. His greatest ability, in a sense, is to go back incessantly on his own past inspirations to unearth them like a necromancer and respire new life into them. His music, like his contrarianism, gives out the sense of being something that keeps running in circles. A snake biting his own tail.

Simon Reynolds has already emphasized this feature of Ariel Pink's artistic vison in his book *Retromania*. The general thesis of the book is that pop culture has stumbled upon an aesthetic dead-end: most of it is obsessed with the past, terminally nostalgic. While the end of the last century was rife with innovation, the early years of the twenty-first century have been characterized, for the most part, by a melancholic nostalgia for those same decades that had just passed. This, of course, has some very nefarious consequences. After all, a culture unable to produce appealing futures is one doomed to a chronic inability to look past itself and imagine what might wait beyond. A culture without escape routes and cursed by a perpetual déjà vu, in other words, or, as the heretical Marxist Paolo Virno has put it:

> The state of mind correlated to déjà vu is that typical of those set on *watching themselves live*. This means apathy, fatalism, and indifference to a future that seems prescribed even down to the last detail. Since the present is dressed in the clothes of an irrevocable past, [...] people must renounce any influence on how the present plays out. It is impossible to change something that has taken on the appearances of memory.

According to Reynolds, Ariel Pink has been one of the main retromaniacs of the 2000s. Pink, with his obsession with quoting and reassembling old styles and past ephemera, has been one of the most refined nostalgics. His music, born out of a kind of constant rumination on his own idols, is the prime example of our *déjà*-vu culture, a sort of haunted house where all the pop things that ever were linger together timelessly. "Without a trace of embarrassment, Ariel describes his sound, woven out of blurry echoes of halcyon radio pop from the sixties, seventies and eighties, as 'retrolicious'. And it is!", says Reynolds:

> Nostalgia is, after all, one of the great pop
> emotions. And sometimes that nostalgia can be
> the bittersweet longing pop feels for its own lost
> golden age. To put that another way: some of
> the great artists of our time are making music
> whose primary emotion is towards other music,
> earlier music.

This characterization is compelling and, for the most
part, correct. But, at least as far as I'm concerned, it
leaves something out. It feels reductive to just call Ariel
Pink nostalgic. It's as if there's something more to his
nostalgism. As if the bigger picture were missing. What
about his contrarianism? And is Pink's retroliciousness just
a nostalgic affair with his past? And what about that whole
outsider glam thing? At the end of the day, it's probably
all a matter of optics: we've witnessed Ariel Pink doing
far more dubious things than Reynolds ever could have
predicted back in 2010, when he published *Retromania*, but
we can no longer just call the weirdness he gave body to
"retromania". Isn't nostalgia quite an idle concept, after
all, for someone this controversial? Nostalgia doesn't cut it
when it comes to the kind of exteriority to the norm Ariel
Pink brings forth. And I have a modest proposal for a better
category for Pink's poetics: Ariel Pink is not nostalgic, he is
paranoid. Paranoia explains his lo-fi escape and the values
he gives a voice to.

Of course, I don't mean paranoia in any clinical sense.
Ariel Pink did not ask me any sort of psychological advice and
I wouldn't just go around diagnosing people I have never met.
When I say "paranoia", I mean it in the anti-clinical sense
that Deleuze and Guattari gave to the term. According to the

ENRICO MONACELLI

two French philosophers, paranoia is a movement of sorts; a dynamic motion an individual or a collective can assume at any given moment in time, just like the ravishing becoming-woman that Marine Girls embodied. But whilst the movement of becoming-woman spreads outwards, the paranoid motion moves inwards: it creates fixed identities, boundaries and, most importantly, it does so by capturing outer material and inscribing repetitions and fixations within them. The paranoid movement quite literally runs in circles onto itself by *overcoding* everything it touches with a predetermined meaning. Needless to say, Deleuze and Guattari were absolutely no fans of the paranoid movement.

While the becoming-woman shakes down the habitual, paranoia reinforces that which is solid by capturing the stuff it finds outside of itself and devouring it in this grand process of rumination and absorption. The heterogeneity of the world is taken in by this all-consuming machine and transformed in homogeneity. Or, as Deleuze and Guattari put it, in extremely convoluted terms: "It is this force of projection that defines paranoia, this strength to start again from zero, to objectify a complete transformation: the subject leaps outside the intersections of alliance-filiation, installs himself at the limit". In plainer terms, it means that the paranoid movement, rather than being an escape *outward*, it's a leap *inwards*. Paranoia sees what's out there and brings it in. If the escapee runs for the exit, paranoia drags the outside in and shuts the doors to the great outdoors. "For the first time, something has been withdrawn from life and from the earth that will make it possible to judge life and to survey the earth from above: a first principle of paranoiac knowledge", as Deleuze and Guattari would put it.

The paranoid movement is, in other words, a way to construct firm identities in the evermoving and everchanging

149

flux of time and culture — "the paranoiac is the subject of the statement that takes itself to be the subject of enunciation". This is the kind of operation that Pink does when he ventures into his archive: he digs deep and then captures whatever he finds. He might be moved by nostalgia, sure, but he's not just contemplating pop's lost golden age. While Marine Girls sought a breakage, Ariel Pink finds himself unwillingly chasing his own tail, repeating the habits he inherited from his past and putting them onto the things he fancies the most. Everything is absorbed, neutralized and homogenized: cock rock is made to become the same as darkwave. While nostalgia idly remembers, the paranoid movement spins round and round, churning new products out whilst Pink is impotently engulfed in his own ghosts, which he sees everywhere. Paranoia freed from its clinical meaning is, I believe, a good explanation for Pink's running in circles and, also, the logical conclusion to the trajectory begun by R. Stevie Moore's outsider glam.

This may sound very esoteric. Perhaps, by making my actual conceptual sources explicit, I might dispel some of the abstract fluff. After all, this interpretation of mine is not something I came up with on my lonesome reading abstruse French philosophy. It actually comes from a rather practical and terrifying book by Franco "Bifo" Berardi called *Heroes*. In the book, Berardi tries to analyse a much more unsettling cultural phenomenon than Ariel Pink's contrarian lo-fi: mass shootings. The reason for undertaking such a daunting task is readily said: mass shooters, like all cultural phenomena with a certain resonance in the collective imagination, are an expression of our shared psychic life. They express something about how our society feels and thinks and lives. Something horrid, of course, but something crucial to our collective experience, precisely in its horror.

Like the moralist philosophers of the seventeenth century, Berardi goes about the squalor and fright of surveying such a topic by creating an emotional bestiary of sorts: he catalogues some of the most common affections and emotions that lead a person to mass slaughter and the most common emotional reactions that mass shootings elicit in our society — the underlying thesis being, again, that these same emotions are things that influence and shape our social life beyond the actual occurrence of a terroristic action. A mass shooting is, in other words, an extreme catalyst to highlight the negative affections and sad passions that course through our capitalist society. Among these feelings, inspired by Deleuze and Guattari's haute political ontology, there's paranoia. And, according to Berardi, "In the last few decades, artistic sensibility has been paralysed by a sense of paranoiac enchantment". I couldn't agree more —Ariel Pink is a glaring example.

The way Berardi describes paranoia is quite straightforward: paranoia, according to him, is the malaise of knowing everything, of a society in perpetual information overload. His chief inspiration is a passage from Jackie Orr's *Panic Diaries*, a genealogy of panic disorder and contemporary society. Orr writes:

> In an exquisite sense of contagious connectivity, paranoia is one form that a felt insistence on the social and historical structuring of psychic experience can take. Paranoia "knows well" the resonant evidence suggesting that everything really is connected, the psyche and the power of the social, a small white pill and a wildly historical story.

Paranoia is, then, a social dynamic that absorbs the heterogeneity of a hyper-connected society and a disorderly world and reduces it to the homogeneity of a pre-existing, controllable knowledge — just as it was for Deleuze and Guattari. It's an inward movement that reduces the Many to a paranoid One. Or, in plainer terms, it is a false sense of experiencing everything as already figured out and controlled in advance. The ultra-chaotic world we live in, already said and done.

For Berardi, the resulting emotional effects of paranoia are twofold, but always tragic: the paranoid subject feels deliriously masterful and impotent. This mastery descends from the feeling of already knowing all there is to know; the impotence arises from the sense that there is nothing besides what is already known. No future, no accidents, no encounters. Only an interminably protracted repetition of the same tropes, ideas, ways of living. The paranoid subject is a sort of sage of his own little cognitive circle: he artfully knows and quotes everything there is to know, but sees no horizon beyond that. "Paranoia 'knows well', but we need to free ourselves from the effects of that knowledge in order to disentangle from it the possibility of invention, of richness, of happiness and the good life", as Berardi aptly describes it.

This description fits Ariel Pink like a glove, more than nostalgia ever could. After all, which pop golden age is he nostalgic for, really? In his songs you could hear echoes of all sorts of pop and unpop music from past decades. Songs like "For Kate I Wait" or "White Freckles" or "Feels Like Heaven" are mashes of the psychedelic Sixties, the cocaine Seventies and the hyper-modern darkness of the Eighties. They are the encyclopaedic exercises of someone who can control and reshape the past of pop music at will, since he knows all there is to know about it — but only the past, of course. Ariel Pink's art is Pynchonesque: a series of connections he himself tangles up and controls. In the background, the desperation of running around the same tracks over and over and over again. And I say that paranoia is a better descriptor for Ariel Pink also because it accounts for the rest of his aesthetic, so to speak: the contrarianism and the completion of what R. Stevie Moore had started.

Paranoia, after all, feeds on spiralling desires and the sort of enjoyment that Ariel Pink's contrarianism elicits is the twisting-and-turning chase of scolder and scoldee. The point of contrarianism is to create commotion and then go back to square one, as if mainstream culture could never change. It's not a genuine attempt to overthrow consensus reality, as desirable as that might be. On the contrary, it's the paranoid reassurance that all one could do is already written prior to any action. The only transgressive thing left is testing the limit of what is already known and then going back to that same sad world.

Ariel Pink's most infamous involvement in politics is a perfect exemplification of this dynamic: nothing really changed and nothing was even meant to change. The goal was to re-instate a president that had already won the previous election. Contrary to other watershed uprisings in the West in recent history, like the war on the streets of Seattle during the WTO's Ministerial Conference or in Genoa during the 2001 G8 summit, there was nothing transformative about the peaceful rallies, nor the riots. There wasn't even the disruptive no-demandism of something like the *Gilets Jeune*. There was just the violent explosion of paranoid desperation: if nothing could ever change, at least give us our favourite president. It is this sort of world-hatred that stems from the conviction of having seen all there is to see and knowing all there is to know. This, clearly, is not the paralysis of nostalgia; it's something far more menacing.

And this spiralling motion extends also to the rest of Ariel Pink's poetics. When talking about R. Stevie Moore, I claimed that his one blind spot was his certitude of being lonely and misunderstood; his thorough pessimism regarding the creation of a community around his music. R. Stevie Moore had utilised lo-fi as a method to cut out any sort of external authority over his expression, but this had also alienated him from the possibility of fulfilling his desire to be recognized and adored — according to him, at least, and despite the community that grew around his musical output. But while R. Stevie Moore blamed his loneliness on his contingent situation — he was ahead of his time, too idiosyncratic to be a pop star, and all that jazz — Ariel Pink made it a stylistic choice. A badge of honour, even. Ever provocative and allegedly misunderstood, despite enormous indie success, Pink has fashioned his creation around the idea that he can't have a crowd cheering him. There's this self-destructive closure to him that just characterizes all he does. Those isolationist tendencies that were an underlying feature of R. Stevie Moore's outsider glam are overblown in Pink's hands. They become an aesthetic choice, and a paranoid one at that. The point is, again, not to build something better, but to enjoy the repetition of what's already there. Horizonless transgression, through and through. The picture is quite clear: Ariel Pink's escape is *inwards*, not *outwards*.

And, obviously, this isolationism, this escape inwards is not a way to break out of the world as we know it. It's not Brian Wilson's psychedelia, Daniel Johnston's Love and Hope, or Marine Girls' becoming-woman. There's nothing alien about this outsideness. It's exactly how Pink himself describes his own music: "familiar and uncanny". It is a reinforcement of the psychic closures that are already in place. But we should ask for something more than this. We should be able to go beyond ourselves and this world. We should not strive to know-it-all, but to forget and discover. Move outwards. Berardi's ethical injunction should lead us forward, outside of this suffocating closure: "Now all this paranoia has to be disposed of [...] Let's forget about it; let's go forward."

You won't b here

Perfume Genius's anal terror

*it seems they were all cheated of some marvellous experience which is not
going to go wasted on me which is why I'm telling you about it*
Frank O'Hara

"There is a big secret about sex: most people don't like it",
wrote Leo Bersani, caustically, at the very beginning of his
seminal *Is the Rectum a Grave?* A showstopping opener, for sure.
And most would, at first, disagree with him whole-heartedly.
It's really hard to find someone who would openly and
unapologetically admit to not liking sex in some way, shape or
form. Not liking an activity that binds a lot of our social ties
and identities and relationships would frankly seem like a hell
of an anti-social statement in the eyes of normal society.

Obviously, Bersani was perfectly aware of the outlandishness
of his one-liner. He had, after all, no sociological data to
back up his idea and, in any case, gathering such data would
have been an impossible feat, regardless of his willingness
or capability to obtain it. "I don't have any statistics to back
this up", he quipped sardonically, "and I doubt (although
since Kinsey there has been no shortage of polls on sexual
behavior) that any poll has ever been taken in which those
polled were simply asked, 'Do you like sex?'" He believed,

nonetheless, that beyond the happy, sociable façade of our sexual lives stood a profound well of silent (and silenced) discomfort. Sex, for Bersani, was a sort of negative pull that tore the fabric of normal life asunder. A destructive energy, so to speak, that constantly undoes our egos, our social contracts and our quietude in the privacy of our bedrooms or wherever else people may be fucking.

This idea is nothing new in contemporary debates on our sexed existence. One could even say that the whole of psychoanalysis, Bersani's field of expertise, is just a beating around this very uncomfortable bush. At least since the publication of Freud's *Civilization and its Discontents*, the thesis that there's something socially disquieting, if not openly anti-social, about sex has been an easily accepted psychoanalytical conceptual pillar. That's ultimately the disturbing fact about the unconscious, after all: you don't really control your deepest desires and sometimes they will break loose, in one way or another. You can knock yourself out trying to be a good, productive citizen, but your sex life won't necessarily comply.

Nonetheless, Bersani made this familiar argument a lot more circumscribed and historically precise. Sure, all sex hides a disquieting force, but some kinds of sex are socially perceived as more dangerous than others. The materiality of our unconscious is built upon the material exclusions and divisions that underpin actually-existing human history. And while straight sex raises, in contemporary society at least, a moderate amount of social anxieties, queer sex unearths a whole ton more. To make matters worse, Bersani wrote his essay around and about a moment in recent history where queer sex was profoundly stigmatized and pathologized: the outbreak of the AIDS epidemic. It was a moment in history when the equation "queer sex = death" was given as natural amongst the silent majority of the capitalist world. And again, while every unconscious is socially troubling, it becomes a lot more unbearable when you are coercively transformed and attacked as some sort of sexual pest.

Bersani, a gay man himself, was nonetheless not that scared of the social death that had fallen upon the lives of many queer people. He was not one to play the role of the victim in his writings, for sure, even in such a heinous climate. The main argument of his infamous essay was, in fact, that the sexual disquiet that queer people produced in the heart of normal society was to be analysed, if not downright cherished by queer people themselves. He even went so far as to proclaim that "it is perhaps necessary to accept the pain of embracing, at least provisionally, a homophobic representation of homosexuality". But why? Why put queer people through this sort of needless pain? The answer, for Bersani, was quite simple: only through normality's greatest sexual fears could one properly comprehend normality's Achilles heel and desire's most terrifying potential. The potential, that is, to abolish the self and crack the enclosures of normal life.

Bersani was convinced that the thing that forced homophobes to shiver in terror when it came to the queers was a phobia we have already encountered previously: the fear of openness and, more practically, penetration. Just like Theweleit's macho Nazis, Bersani's straights were petrified at the mere idea of being made subjects to outer invasions — the "seductive and intolerable image of a grown man, legs high in the air, unable to refuse the suicidal ecstasy of being a woman". The main reason why they were terrified at the thought of someone or something invading them was the unconscious belief that being the penetrated and not the penetrating meant losing control over oneself — giving it up to someone or something external. Or, at the very least, being forced to share and negotiate that same libidinal control with a potentially indefinite number of others. Passivity = de-privatizing one's desire, basically. "To be penetrated is to abdicate power", said Bersani, putting on his straight boy drag, and "women and gay men spread their legs with an unquenchable appetite for destruction". Furthermore, "Male homosexuality advertises the risk of the sexual itself as the risk of self-dismissal, of losing sight of the self", cheered on Bersani. The mere thought of giving up control over the self in the face of another, any other, is unbearable to most and, to Bersani, that was a fear worth exploring and exploding.

Whether this was true or not in a biological or ontological sense, of course, did not matter. This fear functions not due to some biological underpinning — something Bersani nonetheless argued at some point, meeting my most sincere dissent. And penetration is not *really* an abdication of power either, of course. But the phobia of passivity — and, more generally, of control-loss — works, like all phobias, because it lingers unconsciously as an implicit myth that the straights, especially straight men, tell themselves. And if it was really a scary myth and if people still believed it unconsciously, it had to be deployed, believed Bersani, to make our contemporary sexual contradictions short-circuit. To make sexual normality go pop. Rather than taking the liberal approach to self-shattering desire, trying to comfort the silent majority and its discontent with passivity and bottomhood, Bersani proposed a full-on embrace of the things that were more frightening and abhorrent about gay sex. No reconciliation with straightness, then, but full-on anal terror.

One adamant example of this Bersanian logic is one of the sweetest and most lurid lo-fi records of the 2010s: Perfume Genius's *Learning*. Perfume Genius burst onto the scene as soon as 2010 rolled around. Back then, Mike Hadreas, the man behind Perfume Genius, was a mysterious figure, shrouded in pain and disarray. He presented himself black-eyed in mugshot-esque black-and-white photos. His public persona and his artistic project were fixated on an almost gothic vision of queer sex and death. He projected onto the world this image of a twink on the brink — someone who, despite his meagre twenty years in this world, had experienced quite a bit of crime, violence and desire, and sung about it with no filters or preventive warnings. A lo-fi Jean Genet of sorts, if you will. A ghastly image, granted, but one that, I believe, matched and, in the least problematic sense of the word, beautified the harshest aspects of queer life in a straight world. An image hard to look at, but quite hypnotic in all its revealing and shattering darkness. "I spent my whole life hiding from the things that happened to me, to my family and friends", he'd confess later on, reflecting back on that same darkness that inspired his debut record. "The entirety of all these experiences: abuse, addiction, suicide, all that cool stuff, I couldn't bear to look at it".

Learning matched the looks. The record was mostly composed of home-recorded piano ballads, depressing and horny at once. The lo-fi recording and subject-matter of most of the songs made them sound as if the Yellow Brick Road took Elton John places I wouldn't dare go with a gun. They were thirteen great pop songs stripped down to their barest — as Marine Girls taught us. A piano, a voice and little else. The recording was reverb-drenched, making certain passages almost incomprehensible or a little grating on the ears. Hadreas' voice was beautiful, angelic on every track he's present, but the record sounded wilfully dusty, muddled in noise and static. And the violence and lust these songs exuded was only magnified in the noise.

Perfume Genius recorded these songs after coming back home to his mom in Seattle. He had lived in New York City and had fallen victim to addiction — alcohol, mostly, his grand gateway to annihilation, and other, unspecified drugs. The world had gotten too much for him. He needed a break from everything, a way out of the strangling mundanity he had walled himself into. As he got back to his hometown, he started sketching little tunes to encapsulate the violence and desperation and excitations — to reflect upon the maelstrom that had taken over him, depicting it as unfiltered and powerfully as he humanly could. *Learning* clearly bore the mark of this escape from the pains of the city that best represented haute-baroque capitalism. It was emotionally extreme. It sounded like heavy eyelids, sleepless nights and dealing with the most unpleasant side of oneself.

Learning starts with the title-track, an apt mantra for the twenty-first-century capitalist doom generation. The song repeats over and over:

> *No one will answer your prayers*
> *Until you take off that dress*
> *No one will hear all your crying*
> *Until you take your last breath*

The melody is minimal, almost hollow. The song sets the stage for the rest of the album as a sort of minuscule moment of world-building. In the capitalist hellscape that Perfume

Genius paints, a faithful miniature of this world, there are two ways to relevancy and care: exploitation — gritty, horrid, often sexualized in some way but not necessarily — or death. You either take off your dress and sell yourself short or die, otherwise you're invisible and useless and exposed to all sorts of neglect. *Tertium non datur*:

> *Your father before you*
> *And your sister too*
> *Your husband and blah, blah, blah, blah*
> *You.*

There's no time to reflect on this dismal landscape because, from the second song onward, Perfume Genius starts doodling these little figures, abject and heart-wrenching, that populate this sad, sad world and are ravished by a desire that makes them passive and self-less. The first one is quite startling, the most horrifying of them all: Mary Bell, child-killer. In the 1960s, she strangled two young boys in the suburbs of Newcastle upon Tyne. She was ten when she slayed her first victim. She'd tell the boys that they had a sore throat. She'd massage that out of them, she told. She had survived a childhood of sheer abuse and negligence. After her first murder, she and a friend of hers, Norma, broke into their school. They scribbled defiant confessions all over the place. In one of them, she warned *look out there are murders about* — the phrase that would become Perfume Genius's chorus on "Lookout, Lookout".

The song centres mostly on Mary Bell's second victim: Brian Howe, a three-year-old. Howe was brutally strangled, a crude "M" cut into his stomach with a pair of scissors:

But you carved a name
You carved out a name for yourself

The horror story of Mary Bell serves as a sort of archetype for *Learning*: Mary and Brian are both presented as victims of a horrid world, like all the other characters we'll meet along the way. And they incarnate, in the most extreme and violent way possible, the fear of invasion and of control-loss that Bersani talked about when musing on the psychic abjection of penetration. They are, Mary and Brian, the personification of de-subjectification pushed to its outer, mortal edge. Brian *will not be missed, he didn't have a family to begin with.* He is a social void. And Mary, well, is the apotheosis of a child monster — the enemy of all and any social norms, too young to grasp good and evil and too innocent to stain her hands with such gratuitous blood. They are put on stage, backed by a lonely, distorted piano, as the epitome of what this world fears most: being overtaken by a desire so senseless as to cross any social dogma or taboo or common sense, being invaded so murderously as to be found dead in a ditch. The "suicidal ecstasy" Bersani raved on and on about becomes here quite literal with the salient pair of scissors. The anal terror of invasion, at its most horrifying. Stranger danger at its feverish peak. Perfume Genius does not celebrate or glorify Mary's actions, of course; their existence is simply exposed in all its brutality. They are brought forth for us to see and reflect upon, marvelling at the outer wilderness that grows in our own backyard, disturbing our artificial quietude.

After this initial, virulent apex, the album focuses on the ways in which this precise terror haunts queer lives and sex. The next track, "Mr. Peterson", for instance, is a continuation of sorts of the self-loss and annihilation and anal terror explored in "Lookout, Lookout", but taking as the subject of the song a far more sadly mundane tragedy. A terrifying event, granted, but a way more quotidian one in all its undoubtable horror. "Mr. Peterson" is, at its core, a song about an abusive man committing suicide. He's a high school professor. Mike Hadreas' high school professor, to be specific. The two had a sexual relationship, a violent and unambiguously abusive one:

> *My work came back from class*
> *With notes attached of a place and time*
> *Or how my body kept him up at night*

The story is told in broad strokes, emphasizing not so much the prurient details but the feelings of loss and defencelessness and mourning. And there's an overpowering piety that cuts through the muddy recordings. As much as the act is heinous, and Perfume Genius does not stutter when recognizing how fucked up the power and age imbalance was, there's also a fearless exposition of how it feels to be in a position of sheer loss — a loss of autonomy, selfhood and power. A de-victimization of the abused, so to speak, which, of course, does not make the abuser any less of an abuser. It is a de-victimization that, I'd say, is clearly aimed at putting the listener in a position in which love and hate just strip your self out of your chest. Again, the anal terror of giving it all up, of being open and wounded and letting yourself feel it all. And, at least in this case, feeling quite literally penetrated:

> *He let me smoke weed in his truck*
> *If I could convince him I loved him enough*
> *Enough, enough, enough, 'nuff.*

This idea is possibly best exemplified in the horrifying finale. Rather than condemning the abuser outright, Perfume Genius pauses any sort of moral or ethical judgement. The man splatters on the ground as he jumps off a building and Perfume Genius stops us on that very image to feel the totalizing, vertiginous pain he's feeling. Mr. Peterson is not forgiven, but the singer puts himself in the position of mourning him regardless. He takes on an almost Christological and passive stance, suffering the pain of a wicked sinner, despite what he's done to him. A shocking surrender to the teenage void that burns inside him:

> *When I was sixteen he jumped off a building*
> *Mr. Peterson*
> *I know you were ready to go*
> *I hope there's room for you up above*
> *Or down below*

This harsh outstripping of any consolidated self is really the *fil rouge* that unites the songs on *Learning*. Sex is mostly this sort of egoic dissolution throughout the album. Take, for example, "You Won't B Here", a song less narrative-driven and more focused on a general reflection on queer relationships. Here sex and its consequences are, again, unambiguously tied with a loss of anything solid, with invasions and destructions. It's an unbearable thing where no self can last. Sexual relationships are painful affairs and, in this world, they mostly lead to *unloving*, a category of realtion Eva Illouz has analysed thoroughly. And yet, for Perfume Genius — and Bersani, too — we must endure all of this until the end, using all the libidinal power it unleashes and putting ourselves and our selves in the hands of desire's impossible demands. Until we find ourselves desperate and broken and terminally strung out, we have to bear witness and live through it. Sex is pain and self-annihilation — queer sex, in this world, in particular. And that's fine, as long as you thoroughly and sincerely live it:

> *You might not get (What you were promised)*
> *You might be hollow (Under all of the dust)*
> *But you are hurting (Everyone you touch)*
> *And they won't be here (Tomorrow)*

Let it rip, love has such sights to show you.

But why, though? Fine, all this earnest lovesickness might tear down our defences and open us up to a radical reconfiguration of our self, but what gives? Why are we to leave our self behind, and in favour of what? Pain? Misery? After all this emotional grime, this knee-jerk reaction is possibly the most natural one.

And it is a reaction that has been rightfully leveraged against Bersani on many occasions. The queer theorist has invariably met this contestation with scorn. In *Is the Rectum a Grave?*, he openly mocks the "pastoralism" of those, like his archnemesis Michel Foucault or Andrea Dworkin, looking for a "reinvention of sex", as he himself put it. That anal terror is not a liberation from anything, he claims, and putting oneself through the ordeal is just a way to strip desire of all its embellishments. Fuck any and all nice feelings, let the terror loose. The point of this sexual hyper-pessimism is "the inestimable value of sex as — at least in certain of its ineradicable aspects — anticommunal, antiegalitarian, antinurturing, antiloving". But these conclusions are not Perfume Genius's. Despite depicting the same libidinal darkness Bersani so cheerfully embraces, Perfume Genius still clings to the idea that sex could be good tomorrow — despite the pain and whatever this world claims. I seldom but emphatically used the term "love" while talking about *Learning* precisely for this reason: the point of the record is, at the bottom of it all, love renewed, beyond and above the misery that still rules everything around us, outside of the quotidian reality of capitalist sexual violence.

Consider, for example, "Write to Your Brother", another track telling a scant little story about a girl, eerily called, once again, Mary. This time Mary is just someone Perfume Genius knows presumably well. She has a recovering brother — from what is never specified — and a presumably alcoholic mother. The singer simply urges Mary to write to her brother again, who is far away or locked up somewhere:

> *Mary, you should write to your brother*
> *Every night until he recovers*
> *In the letter press a fresh flower*
> *And bless it with a higher power.*

Despite the bleakness and the recurring fact that the protagonists are broken selves torn asunder by their social class, sex and addictions, the overarching message is one of hope and care. The atrocity exhibition serves as a launching pad to urge Mary, and us in turn, to take care of those around us, no matter how cruel or devastating this world and their desires are. Yes, the bleakness within and without should not be embellished, and Perfume Genius certainly does not do that, but the darkness should be the building ground for a community of lovers that knows nothing of the rules and drudgeries of capital. A godless injunction to "love thy neighbour".

This progression from Bersanian anal terror to radical love shouldn't really be a surprising or contentious characteristic of Perfume Genius's poetics. If we circle back to the opening title track, it becomes quite apparent that this sort of dialectic is in motion from the get-go. In fact, after the depressing mantra about the state of this world, Perfume Genius jumps straight into an almost frightening intimation:

> *But you will learn*
> *to mind me*
> *and you will learn*
> *to survive me*

After all this destruction, our profoundest fear will lead you to this: to learn how to take care of me and how to survive all of this. The desperation here is not blocked out or negated but uplifted to new heights. It becomes, against Bersani's smug nihilism, the necessary motor to reinvent the way we live together.

In this sense, Perfume Genius embodies the theory and idiosyncrasies of one of Bersani's aforementioned nemeses: Andrea Dworkin. She was a radical feminist who received, over time, quite a bit of bad press. She was firmly against pornography, which she saw as a spectacularization of women's submission to men, and she wrote a scandalous book in which she supposedly claimed that all penetrative sex is rape. Contrapoints, the famous leftist YouTuber, once called her the "feminist blackpill", and much of the general public did not receive her any better. She is, to most talking about her in passing or extensively, a killjoy, a moralist, a bigot or simply annoying. Even Bersani, a surprisingly acute reader of her mistreated work, couldn't prevent himself from calling her outright "unhinged". But as much as her posterity berated her, she still stands as one of the greatest thinkers of love and a feminist whose works, as Amia Srinivasan put it, "do matter", since

> they contain certain truths, of the kind many women recognise as they hear them, about the bewildering ubiquity of sexual violence, the lie this violence gives to the promise of women's equality, and the continuities between the most grotesque aspects of women's treatment at the hands of men and the more quotidian assaults on dignity with which nearly all women are intimately familiar.

Dworkin was a writer of both fiction and non-fiction. In her novels, she would depict the violence and joy of sex life as a woman in a straight and patriarchal world, not unlike how Perfume Genius does in his lo-fi ballads. In her essays, she would extend that same rich and ambiguous experience with a prose so commanding that any writers of the past century would pale in comparison. She surely had some extreme positions and, like all good books of ethics and politics, some of the points she made are open to our contemporary revision. Nonetheless, the basic thesis uniting all of her work is clear-cut and still more than relevant.

Her most vital idea, one that strenuously survives in Perfume Genius's music, was that love was to be radically remade. Contrary to Bersani's umbilical sexual nihilism, she was for a sort of concrete utopianism: a utopianism that does not negate the reality of this world but which, nonetheless, advocates for a radical exit from its sexual soot and grime. Once, for example, while analysing James Baldwin's queer intimacies, she wrote:

> Inside an unjust, embittering social universe where there are moral possibilities, however imperilled, of self-esteem and empathy, fucking is the universal event, the point of connection, where love is possible if self-knowledge is real; […] And crossing on that high and rotting and shaking bridge to identity, with whatever degree or quality of fear or courage, is the ordeal that makes empathy possible: not a false sympathy of abstract self-indulgence, a liberal condescension; but a way of seeing others for who they are by seeing what their own lives have cost them.
>
> In fucking, one's insides are on the line.

And this is Perfume Genius's point, I believe, and the reason why he could sing so comfortably about the worst aspects of love under capitalism, still cunningly avoiding falling in Bersani's trap. To Perfume Genius, and Dworkin too, fucking is a dangerous crossing, which has both the power to destroy and generate unexpected communities of care and proximity. The terror that haunts our wet dreams, that fatal passivity that serves as a premonition of the inconvertible fact that you or I or we won't be here tomorrow, is neither negated nor swiftly pacified. His stripped-down ballads, both nihilistic and eerily hopeful, are snapshots of the necessary ambiguity that lies at the heart of any ethics or politics that refuses to do away with the darkness — the thin red line between utopia and annihilation. Letting go of the self through our desires will be necessary if we want this cruel world to be no more. But in the name of fleshy new horizons finding their way into existence. Not death.

From his second album onwards, Perfume Genius gradually abandoned lo-fi and, at least in my eyes, the intensity that underpinned *Learning*. *Put Your Back n 2 It*, his second record, was still rough, both sonically and thematically, but it was also a much tamer endeavour. Still soulful and openly invested in expressing love's impossible demands, but a little posher and more refined. Leaving lo-fi behind and, in turn, the practical sabotage of pop's modes of production, Perfume Genius's music became something far more digestible, less explosive. But the ghost of sexual unrest unearthed by *Learning* still roams the halls of our most intimate hideouts.

A throat being torn open over and over, but beautifully like howling wind

Phil Elverum's outside

> *Living on borders and in margins, keeping intact one's shifting and multiple identity and integrity, is like trying to swim in a new element, an "alien" element. There is an exhilaration in being a participant in the further evolution of humankind, in being "worked" on.*
> Gloria Anzaldùa

Art is for getting rid of yourself. It is a technique — meticulous, carefully calculated — to tear you asunder and let something exterior, something other in. You may not want it or mean it but, as you make art, it gnaws at you, it dissolves what you had been prior. Writing, recording music, painting: if done right, they are all ways to forget and reimagine the bounds of existence. To flee the possible, aiming at the improbable.

Maurice Blanchot was the philosopher who, more than any other, believed in this idea. Art, he thought, is a form of self-reflection that snuffs out the self that it reflects upon. The artist, according to Blanchot, suspends their whole life in their work, upending whatever they were before commencing the process. "This existence is an exile in the fullest sense: we", the humans seen in the glow of artistic defacement, "are not there, we are elsewhere, and we will never stop being there". The end result of art-making, he concludes, is the great unknown beyond. A space where new possibilities become real and present. When talking about literature, for example, he'd say that "the word acts not as an ideal force but as an obscure power, as an incantation that coerces things, makes them really present outside of themselves". Literature — and by proxy, I add, all art — works like sorcery for Blanchot, a veritable dark art: it eliminates what you used to be, leads to unfathomable pathways.

This idea might seem rather maximalist. Art as a technique to make things "present outside of themselves": that is indeed a lot to take in. But it is a rather useful idea when it comes to artists who actually used their art to upend the material conditions of their existence altogether. Like Phil Elverum, who went on a literal exile to write his lo-fi masterpiece, *Dawn*. By the time he recorded *Dawn*, Phil Elverum, the man behind Mount Eerie, was a sort of indie golden standard. He had already produced a slew of masterpieces and great records and pushed the boundaries of what a lo-fi indie record could actually do, both in sound and conceptual scope. Under the moniker Mount Eerie he had put out no-fi gems like *Eleven old songs of Mount Eerie* and *No Flashlight*, for example. But the most well-known among his successful experiments is surely *The Glow pt. 2*, an album Elverum recorded under his previous moniker, the Microphones. Despite its DIY recording, *The Glow pt. 2* sounds gigantic and unprecedented. Elverum used unusual sounds — his movements in the studio, chairs creaking, amps strained to their limits, fingers slapping against his guitar, dissonant backing vocals — to construct these soaring sonic architectures, both improbable and absolutely flawless. The whole album was constructed so masterfully, it is still hard not to be utterly shocked at first exposure. The songs are layered, complex, and the whole sound of the Microphones was astonishingly idiosyncratic and personal. They were all equally catchy compositions, but in mysterious and non-linear ways. On *The Glow pt. 2*, Elverum perfected his unique singing style as well: a mix of good ol' Americana, heartfelt whispering and the muted noises emitted by a guy humming with his neck bent in unnatural positions. And the lyrics, oh the lyrics! They were cryptically heart-breaking, transmuting Elverum's lived experience in impossible riddles. Riddles so hieratic that lovesick Tolkienian elves could have easily sung them:

> *But there's no hope for me, I've been set free*
> *There's no breeze*
> *There's no ship on my sea.*

God, the shivers!

The impact *The Glow pt. 2* had on indie culture at large is hard to overstate. The cover itself, with that bizarre elephant strolling through a colourful landscape, became a meme on any imageboard and forum devoted to indie music. Covers and tributes abound. The influence was so ubiquitous and all-encompassing that Lil Peep, possibly one of the most important figures in contemporary trap music, went so far as to sample bits and pieces of *The Glow pt. 2* in some of his most iconic songs: "White Wine", "Beamer Boy" and "OMFG". *The Glow pt. 2* was veritably the *Sgt. Pepper* of lo-fi music. It broke indie history in half, changing the shape of what indie music could aspire to be before and after its publication.

In comparison, *Dawn* was a much more minimal endeavour. The songs are not layered nor very complex. On the contrary, they are disarmingly simple. Voice and acoustic guitar. All of Elverum's idiosyncrasies are still present, of course, but backed up by hollow, barren arrangements. All of this notwithstanding — or precisely for this sonic nakedness, I'm not entirely sure — *Dawn* is, at least to me, even more breath-taking. Almost unbearable at times, even, in its constant confrontation with what Phil Elverum refers to as the *great ghosts of my life*.

The album is a protracted meditation — honest, above all else, and ecstatic too — on physically fleeing the misery of the modern, capitalist world and what toll and wonders escaping actually, practically entails. Many have compared it to *Walden*, but I think that the comparison is surprisingly an understatement or, at the very least, a distortion. Yes, just like Thoreau, Elverum eschews some brilliant insights on materially living on the liminal edge of capitalist civilization. But it is also a far more contemporary reflection and polemic, in a sense. While Thoreau, at the end of the day, had the ambition of speaking about life in the wild universally and eternally, Elverum sang and wrote (the album is accompanied by a 140-page-long *Winter Journal*) about *our* life in *our* wild. Elverum's insights speak to and about us in particular; they bear the mark of our historical conjunction — something no Thoreau nor Kerouac, for that matter, could have done, for obvious, temporal reasons. *Dawn* is an assault against our life as it stands *now*, in the twenty-first century, not somewhen else.

Elverum wrote *Dawn* in exile. After a nasty breakup, he figured he had to flee the world. His exit from our capitalist mundanity happened between 2002 and 2003. The Bush Jr. administration was at its feverish peak at the time. The social immiseration the neo-con regime had imposed on American life was obviously a key factor in his decision to escape. His private pain was impossible to withstand and elaborate in a world turning so rapidly into a securitarian, fully privatized, right-wing dystopia. In an economic system in which everything rotted under the merciless grind of production, consumption and war, human life could not flourish in any meaningful sense. He left to claim his existence back and suck life's marrow outside the grasp of the State, the Law and the Market. He lived in a cabin in the woods in Norway. There he read Tolstoy incessantly and he started penning down the impressions that the wild, void of all humans, imposed on his senses. Once a year passed, he had on his hands a hefty chunk of meditations, ruminations, songs. *Dawn* is all set in this existential outer interregnum.

The record starts precisely with a scene ripped out of this wilderness:

> *I'll go gather wood*
> *What I do I'll do good*

In the frostbitten Norwegian emptiness, Elverum starts *Dawn* by presenting himself immersed in a life absolutely alien to our alienated normality under capitalism. He is mostly alone. He doesn't have to punch in and out of some bullshit job. He's gathering wood and surviving in conditions that we, the normals, would probably consider extreme or even insane. But rather than romanticizing this same extremity or indulging in some Unabomber-esque primitivist fantasy, he starts looking for justifications for his actions. Why is he there? What led him to abandon everything and move to the middle of nowhere? What's the motive behind the need to flee the world as it currently stands? He is no hero or adventurer, after all; just a simple man with rather simple ambitions and needs. And the answer is, again, rather simple but existentially rich: face grief and be faithful to the promise of a better life. He is not there to find a more authentic self or something like that. His retreat is aimed at disrobing old habits and taking up new ones. And making space for a life more attuned to his true desires, beyond the discontent our contingent situation has built up for us. Only a radical secession from our current cultural climate and its traps could do that for him:

> *It was my own heart that led me there*
> *It was the way I saw wolves' tracks*
> *Left the lair and just went back*
> *It was my new baby stare*

The fact that he is taking the time to self-reflect upon why he chose to do all of that is interesting in and of itself. Throughout this genealogy of lo-fi music, I have often stressed the idea that lo-fi is not a naïve or "simpler" genre. On the contrary, it is a conscious, critical decision; an experiment with art and existence. In this sense, it is meaningful that Elverum would ask himself and the listener why he even did any of this to begin with: it shows just how unnatural such a choice is. Both recording a lo-fi record and going into exile from the capitalist world are critical moves that put the normality of how things usually run into question, albeit at a glaringly different degree. *Why did I do this? Why did others not?* Normal behaviours are probed and questioned. There's nothing "natural" or "authentic" in any of this. On the contrary, the natural and the given are suspended and abandoned.

And with Elverum, this critical gesture embedded in the act of doing lo-fi recording takes on an even more drastic meaning. "Why am I doing this?" exposes, in a sense, the cost of critique and brings us back to the Blanchotian idea that art defaces the artist leading him to the unknown. The fact that Elverum stops and wonders what he's doing is meaningful because it is an honest exposition of what radical critique feels like. Suspending everything around him, he is faced with the abyss that comes after the flood. If nothing is normal and nothing is given, what am I doing?

And this opening song, "It Wasn't the Hunting", encapsulates perfectly the message that lo-fi and critique take on in Elverum's hands: the will to suspend normality and the anguish of not having a stable footing anymore. He recorded his albums with poor means, nurturing as much as he can his own expressive freedoms in extreme emotional and, sometimes, geographical conditions in order to sever any ties with normality's grind — to suspend the onwards march of history and capital. The Marxist catastrophist Walter Benjamin once wrote that, "Marx says that revolutions are the locomotives of history. But perhaps it is quite otherwise, perhaps revolutions are an attempt by passengers on this train — namely the human race — to activate the brake", and to Elverum, music was, on a more minor scale, just that: an emergency brake we activate to block the existence of an unjust reality. DIYing an album meant, for Elverum, being faithful to a wild interzone, both psychic and physical, in which an exit from compulsions and constrictions is still both possible and desirable. A space where, through a ruthless, practical critique of everything that is, new ways of living and loving and dying could be expressed and practiced, albeit with no guarantees or fixed forms to hold on to. The joy and terror of critique.

This existential place outside the world of capitalism and its norms is not unaffected by the present condition. On the contrary, it communicates constantly with its present, setting up this painful back and forth between how life is on the outside and the inside. Elverum's escape is not ahistorical; it's always a retreat *from* what the world actually is like. This tireless communication is often present on *Dawn*. The most tragic example is surely "With My Hands Out", on which Elverum imagines his return to the universe of his previous existence: his past relationship, the relationships he entertained with the world, his life before his unmooring:

> *I want to go back*
> *Across that sea*
> *With my hands up*
> *I want to come back from this robbery*
> *With my hands up, with my hands up*
> *And I will lie down and be handcuffed*
> *Take me, I will be yours*
> *Dripping wet*
> *Just try and hold me*
> *I am dripping wet and limp*

He hallucinates coming back like a criminal, a deserter. Being captured and cuffed. And, again, avoiding any primitivist fantasies, he wonders whether his previous life would love him again, hold him for good. He airs out all the doubts and pain that come with such a radical break. The guilt of leaving everything behind. The haunting possibility, embedded in every revolutionary movement, that this was all a mistake. The hallucination culminates in "Wolly Mammoth's Mighty Absence", a song solely centred around the end of his *holy night* of exile:

> *I know day is dawning now, so ends my holy night*
> *It's back to the world I go, back to the girls and shows*
> *And other worldly woes, and their unfurling flows*
> *Will I carry myself slowly enough to remember?*
> *I sit on a dark rock doing nothing still, just crowded*
> *And there's the love in flesh and bone.*

Will *the gold digger, underground* even remember the treasures he found in his run for a better life? The prospect of fully surrendering hangs there, like a threat or a redemption, according to the difficulties and the joys the jailbreak brings.

But the treasures are truly there, nonetheless, whatever the outcome might be. And on *Dawn*, there are moments of pure affirmation, sheer victory against drudgery and boredom and capitalist domestication. To name just one: "I Said 'No'", the most lyrical ode to unmooring I've ever heard.

The song is a dialogue. On one side, a general *some people*, and on the other, Phil, completely transfigured by his experiences on the outside. The song goes:

> *Some people say: "Arise! Arise! Arise! Live friend live!"*
> *I say: "Die."*
> *I say: "Shade yourself."*
> *I say: "Shine what precious light you have into caves*
> *And when it dies out, stay in there."*
> *I say: "find life where you foolishly saw graves."*

Elverum openly and unabashedly affirms this little death of his as a full embrace of the thickness of reality. Where others would advise getting far from the intensity of the Real, Elverum sings for those who senselessly go further beyond. "Stay there, with your finitude and the great, vast, uncaring outdoors" is the basic ethical tenet. And you don't have to go to Norway or some other woods to do that, don't worry! You just have to accept the concrete present you already live in, its breaming possibilities and its unbearable realities. That volcanic concreteness beneath the abstract moralities and productive imperatives and meaningless futures this world puts before our eyes to keep our servitude in place and our freedoms unthinkable. The concreteness of your existence entirely, that is: the fact you'll die and love and be a myriad of things you'd never even considered. Only a fraction of these experiences will be productive or meaningful or morally justifiable, and all of those things that will fall under these categories will be probably the least intense or worthwhile.

The last verse is powerfully truncated:

> *There's a ringing in my ears that's faint and high*
> *And when I listen close to it, it says…*

It leaves the listener in absolute silence. In the midst of whatever is actually humming or whispering or shouting around him. In the dense concrete engulfing them.

In such intense conceptual and musical moments, Elverum voices the most radical proclamations in contemporary philosophy. A proclamation of belligerent intents that echoes throughout modernity, shouted or whispered by the most intransigent radicals. A declaration of war that was uttered for the first time in Nietzsche's theory-fictional fantasy, *Thus Spoke Zarathustra*. In that book, Nietzsche laid out clearly one of the most powerful maxims for all of those who sought a new world. It reads:

> I beseech you, my brothers, remain faithful to the earth, and do not believe those who speak to you of otherworldly hopes! Poison-mixers are they, whether they know it or not. Despisers of life are they, decaying and poisoned themselves, of whom the earth is weary: so let them go.

As is often the case with Nietzsche, the meaning of this quote is quite sibylline and many reactionaries have interpreted it as a stale and limp injunction to "reject modernity, embrace tradition". The proper meaning of it, or at least the most powerful and resonant one, if read correctly and recklessly, couldn't be further from that, though. It is no "Blut und Boden", where the Earth and human identity (always white, always male, always "normal") coincide perfectly and reinforce one another. In that passage, on the contrary, Nietzsche is urging the reader to remain faithful to the concreteness of their existence and to experiment with one's own existence. Ditch any sort of ulterior authority or article of faith, he says, and believe in the actual life that courses through you, especially in those moments when lived experience would lead you to find new and freer ways of being — when it would lead you, in other words, to *something* that exceeds you and how you thought the world could actually be.

It is, in a sense, an ode to reckless critique: bracket all costumes and mores, everything normal and natural, and escape towards the open beyond. There's no god up above and no boss could ever lead you to any solid truth. The earth, contrary to the State's land and capital's property, knows no enclosure and exceeds any fixity. Dwell and expend that borderlessness, that earthly freedom from all limits and certainties as much as you possibly can, says Nietzsche. Or, as Deleuze would vertiginously put it, commenting on this very passage: "A will of the Earth, what would a will capable of affirming the Earth be like? What does it want, this will without which the Earth itself remains meaningless? What is its quality, a quality which also becomes the quality of the Earth? Nietzsche replies: 'The weightless…'". Despite the insecurity and lack of any pacified, pre-made way of life, this is ultimately the only state in which anything is still possible. The only condition where all futures are weightless and achievable.

Dawn finishes on another truncation. The last song, "Goodbye Hope", is quite esoteric and wilfully open-ended. On it, Elverum says goodbye to both his old self and, cryptically, hope too — what he used to be and what he hoped he could have been. He sheds his old skin and finds himself capable of living through darkness and pitch-black night, despite not knowing exactly what he will become next. From this moment onward, no one can say what will become of Elverum. He lets darkness in, and fear as well:

> *Hello darkest fear, goodbye eyes-closed*
> *In the lonely, lonely, lonely night*
> *In the long shadows*
> *I fell to my knees in tears*
> *And said "Sweet Heart, hello"*

The echo of his broken heart rings amidst a wider state of unrest and freedom and dread. Anyone looking for a thorough answer to the doubts, the victories, the tears is left frustrated by a song that keeps the ending suspended, up for grabs:

Hello my heart, and yes, goodbye Hope
You know we will go steady
Say "Goodbye" and "No"
You'll find me fanning out my warm unfolding hands
Blindly let me go

Is it surrender? A declaration of permanent revolution? In this state of unknowing and uncertainty, left to our own devices, we are abandoned to our own freedom. It is our turn, now, to flee.

At the very end of *Being and Nothingness*, Sartre wrote a critique of the dull, voluntary obedience most people embrace when confronted by the prospect of revolt and freedom. It wasn't the most sophisticated critique of all time, granted, but it was extremely effective, and it echoed, in accessible terms, Nietzsche's almost mythological prose. He wrote:

> Man seeks being blindly, hiding from himself the free project in which this search consists; he makes himself such that the tasks placed along his path *await* him. Objects are silent demands, and in himself he is nothing but a passive obedience to these demands.

Or, in other words, modern humanity — or, maybe, for Sartre, humanity in general, but that sounds quite ahistorical and non-Marxist to me — seeks the reassurance of the Law and the Good; of stuff that's already fixed and valuable that tells them where to go and what to do and why. But this belief in a Good that is already given and natural and already out there is what he called *bad faith*: a paper-thin dogma to keep the reality of freedom out of sight. The only thing that it's already out there is the black hole of freedom — the bustling possible forms the cosmos might eventually assume.

Existentialism, Sartre's philosophical credo, was, on the contrary, a shattering of this belief:

> ontology and existential psychoanalysis (or the spontaneous and empirical application that men have always made of these disciplines) must show the moral agent that he is the being through whom values exist. At that point his freedom will become conscious of itself and discover itself in anguish as the unique source of value, and the nothingness through which the world exists. As soon as the quest for being and the appropriation of the in-itself become disclosed as its possibles, freedom will apprehend, through and in anguish, that these are possible only against the ground of the possibility of other possibles.

In simpler terms, Sartre urged his readers to be faithful to reality as it is, not the Good or the Law or, even, Capital. There's freedom(s) out there and revolt is yours to make. The earth is brimming with possibilities and forking pathways for you to run down. Lives you never even considered are really there for you to create.

In his music, especially *Dawn*'s glacial climates and absolute unrest, Mount Eerie made himself an heir to this vision. His art and exile tore normality out of him, leading him to experiment with the varieties of freedom he could conjure up with his poor means. His music is a testament to the efficaciousness of his earthly faith: the grandeur of the unsure and the fugitive.

Epilogue: Coughing up blood at McDonald's

*DSBM trap, the death of guitar music
and the future of lo-fi*

*You don't really understand the importance, but sometimes when I drive
through these streets at night I can smell the pain of all these people
living in here. I can smell how all these people are just… trapped in
their lives… Their day-to-day life…*
A weirdo in Harmony Korine's *Trash Humpers*

Two kids in the American suburb. One wears a black T-shirt
with the three masks of the serial killers from the slasher flick
The Strangers. They creep on top of containers and abandoned,
post-industrial spots. The video is now unavailable. The
two kids fell out and took it down. Re-uploads, nonetheless,
abound. In the video, they rap with a deadbeat tone over
a minimal, lo-fi trap beat — a beat blown-out to the point
of sounding like black metal. The song is called "Nevada".
The synths buzz like broken chainsaw and one of the kids,
Sematary, his *nom de guerre*, moans *AAAAAAAA* to start the war
dance. On the song, he drops some of most effective suburban
horror I've heard in a while, both chilling and cartoonish:

ENRICO MONACELLI

I been rockin' back and fuckin' forth in the corner
I been getting super fuckin' gone 'til the mornin' (Ahh)
You believe in life, you're a dumb motherfucker
If you really wanna try, we will run you over
I been coughing up blood, dyin' at McDonald's
I been mixing Benadryl and Tussin in my Monster
(In my monster)
I'm glad the world's burnin', I believe in monsters

He has an army of Skellingtons at his command, he claims. Are they Jack Skellington's relatives? Who knows... The other kid, Ghost Mountain, doubles down on the horror and emptiness: *Nothing left but the hum crawlin' out the hills.* In the chorus, the two of them, Ghost Mountain and Sematary, sing *I keep a cutter like the Nevada*, a threat that will surely sound meaningless to those not exhibiting any sort of internet brain-rot. (Nevada refers to a macabre meme that spread on 4chan around 2004. The meme mostly featured a Japanese girl wearing a sweater sporting the word "Nevada", hence the nickname the internet assigned to her was Nevada-tan. She stabbed some of her classmates to death with a boxcutter.) These two rappers are the face of lo-fi in our post-internet age.

My genealogy of lo-fi has been, thus far, quite untimely. Concentrating mostly on guitar music, I have glossed over the fact that, well, guitar music is dead. Or, at the very least, not doing great. The music market at large has shapeshifted under the pressure of online piracy, streaming platforms and the ubiquitous availability of personal computers, which have democratized access to music-making tools. Free software and VSTs have made the outsider glam dreams of myriad bedroom rockstars a reality. And the music we consume has, in turn, changed drastically. On the one hand, global music

187

has become more fragmented than ever. With each listener lost in their Spotify echo-chamber, it is quite hard to say what is trendy or up-to-date and what isn't. It is even hard to say what is actually mainstream anymore. On the other hand, a lot of popular music in this new patchwork environment has become more "digital" and less guitar-driven. The popularity of trap, for example, attracting and inspiring a lot of young musicians, is a testament to this shift in music production. Even genres that fell under the purview of some shade of rock have become thoroughly computer-based, so to speak. Which is not bad, of course: why buy expensive instruments when you can make all the sounds they ever could on your PC, right?

My choice of avoiding confronting the present situation until now is twofold. Firstly, I believe that ruins are to be cherished. Not for nostalgia's sake, but because their decrepit nature serves as a counterpoint to the suffocating totality of the present. Things have been otherwise, the past holds so many secret doorways to futures that could-have-been. Focusing on outmoded things serves as a reminder that the present is just one contingency among many that did not happen. Secondly, and more importantly, I believe that the thesis that runs through my analysis of lo-fi still stands even in a more contemporary and extended context. Even if I took into account the various and more up-to-date versions of lo-fi that have appeared over the years, my point wouldn't vary. After all, lo-fi is not a musical genre, I claimed, but a teenage interzone, a sabotage. And if it is really this very practical, reckless critique of how things should go when producing music, it shouldn't really matter whether it is applied to trap or indie music.

Sematary is an outstanding example of this idea, I believe. The lineage that inspired his music is extremely varied. His main influence comes from trap and drill music; a virulent, lo-fi kind of trap, underground and hostile. Black Kray, Chief Keef, Gucci Mane — artists who have, in different ways and under different guises, defended a staunch DIY ethics and a lo-fi sound. Rough samples, homemade productions and ugly recordings. From this kind of trap music, he revives every nasty detail: the obsession with True Religion, the brand that all of his crew, called Haunted Mound, wears and that was all the rage during the g(l)ory days of early trap music; the loud, obnoxious DJ tags spliced throughout the tracks; an unhealthy love for Makatussin. Furthermore, this precise strain of trap music has produced various techniques of sonic ruination, which all play a crucial role in Sematary's sound: bass-boosting, chopping-and-screwing and many other defacements. All of these guerrilla remix tactics play a crucial role in making Sematary's music gruesome and, at points, unbearable.

On top of this lineage, outer influences too. Black metal is the most prominent, with its screeches and no-tech, hard-line, lo-fi attitude. Sematary has sampled many black metal bands in his songs, from Woods of Desolation to Lifelover. On one song, he even sings *hot girl she like BDSM/you know me, I like DSBM*, an acronym that stands for Depressive Suicidal Black Metal and indexes a particularly bleak and raw black metal subgenre.

But the more *extreme* side of lo-fi indie rock, closer to the music analysed in this book, is an influence on his music as well. To name just one example, on one of his first underground hits, "Pain", Sematary sampled Xiu Xiu, an experimental rock band that has toyed with lo-fi quite a bit in their career. Sematary covers basically the whole spectrum of lo-fi music in his sound. A tendency that is, in and of itself, endemic to the digital native zeitgeist and would have probably been wholly incomprehensible to the lo-fi artists of the late twentieth or even early twenty-first century: being always one click away from the whole global aesthetic canon, it is ridiculous and indefensible to restrict oneself to one genre. "Steal wherever you can and mutate everything you touch" is the name of the game in the post-internet world. Even on a merely visual level, Sematary extends the phantasy that lo-fi culture at large has weaved about in his various non-musical mutations. His music videos are a hybrid of Harmony Korine's VHS demonism, the most blatantly lo-fi filmmaker to ever live, and Tobe Hooper's American nightmares. Imagine an unholy union of *Gummo* and *Texas Chain Saw Massacre*, begetting the ultimate poor image. The protagonists of his songs are all hillbilly monster kids at odds with the whole world. On one song, "Truey Jeans", he samples a whole dialogue from Korine's infamous *Trash Humpers*.

But even with all these influences and mutations, mostly alien to the artists in my genealogy, the point, the ethical baseline of Sematary's sonic craft remains basically the same: his music is a luddite action against pop's machinic hidden reverse. A sabotage of how music-production normally works, thoroughly obsessed with how we can break and hack the machines we use to make sounds. This is most apparent in his most extreme and accomplished record thus far, *Rainbow Bridge 3*. The album is a lethal blend of all his most outrageous influences: every sample is lifted from some dank DSBM track; the bass is boosted to the verge of the unlistenable; Sematary shouts most of the time. It is pure DSBM trap, a horrid sonic experiment meant to test just how much you're able to stomach. Sonically, it's pretty obvious that the point is to mess with music at a structural level: gain new forms of expression through a radical action on how everything in the album is recorded. And the lyrics are grotesquely violent too, just to enhance the power of the poor sounds. They depict, in over-the-top, splatterpunk terms, a dilapidated post-industrial world, made ugly and terrifying by our current way of being. And among the many blood splatters and chainsaw deliriums, there are also rare moments of political finesse, like *Imma slap a Proud Boy/Imma slap a transphobe*, clear indication of a healthy hatred of all fascistic control. The music itself, with its pulp poetics, remains the sound of a teen revolt never exhausted. The point is always the same: attack the machine, destroy this reality.

Sematary might be an egregious example, even an especially nasty one, but he's surely not alone. He is just one of the figures that populate the lo-fi digital underground. Contemporary music is dotted with figures, prominent or parochial, that have cultivated a fascination with lo-fi's sabotage, like Yung Lean and Bladee, with their angelic auto-tune defacements of the human voice, for example. Or, again, 100 gecs or Jane Remover, with their grating hyperpop packed with the virulent poor sounds of the virtual worlds. Or sewerslvt's alienated, Lain-pilled junglism. Or Parannoul's and Weatherday's otherworldly emogaze. Or Asian Glow's digital dream pop. Or the plastic tropicalism of a label like Artetetra. Or the frost-bitten extravaganza of Grime Stone Records, another label that has been venturing into the weirdest recess of dungeon synth and black metal's lo-fi for a while now. Saboteurs are everywhere.

Speaking of Grime Stone Records, I think it is only fair to ponder a bit on how radical and unmarketable lo-fi music can get in the midst of our *extreme present*. Grime Stone Records is solely specialized in putting out tons of confounding records, mainly inspired by two ultra-niche genres in contemporary music: raw black metal and dungeon synth. Raw black metal, on the one hand, is a subgenre of black metal, the infamous strain of extreme metal born in Norway in the 1990s. Raw black metal is characterized by the fact that it is, indeed, rawer than regular black metal: underproduced, rough around every conceivable edge, just plain nasty. What is dungeon synth, on the other hand, is much harder to explain. It is still a spin-off of black metal, in the sense that it was first conceived within the black metal scene. Nonetheless, it is not metal at all. It is a synth-driven genre. The best way to describe it would be: the *Lord of the Rings* soundtrack played on an old Casio and recorded in the worst way conceivable. It is music made for D&D nights in an attic in some forgotten region of the world.

It is safe to say that neither of these genres sell out stadiums, nor very small venues. They are niche, and proudly so. But on top of these already unmarketable foundations, Grime Stone Records puts their own extremely weird twist. Their records sport a staunch fidelity to an unmistakeable queer sensibility, and they're also nerdy beyond belief: raw black metal albums dedicated to Elizabeth Bathory's femininity or 8-bit dungeon synth records or just weird hybrids that traverse the whole rainbow of possibilities offered by the outer fringes of these already fringe genres.

Just like Sematary, these unholy crossings are mostly possible because of the digital world we live in. When hyper-connectedness is the name of the game, uniting disparate things and experimenting in unruly manners is only logical. But again, the lo-fi ethos of Grime Stone Records turns this virtual unholy crossing into full-fledged sabotage. Being the product of a few people doing things themselves, these records are time-travelling agents smuggling in artefacts from a world in which market-logic is not a concern anymore. Cutting out any form of exterior authority, lo-fi lets the secret conspirators behind Grime Stone Records do their own thing, as if this world was no longer. Thanks to the tools of present capitalism, something as weird as Grime Stone Records is, in a sense, allowed to exist in the first place. After all, the hyper-connectedness of our present gives them the means to find outer inspirations coming from unthinkable places. Moreover, it helps them find the improbable small crowd who would love their unspeakable magick. But their sonic craft is the real key to behaving, aesthetically speaking, as if the pressure of the capitalist world was no longer.

Ditching the studio-industrial complex still means being able to express the particularity of one's existence without the bounds and constraints of the music-market. This amphibian position is rather interesting because it practically enacts a form of social engagement that does not shy away from how the world actually is but, at the same time, refuses its logic in the name of a world yet to come — a proper postcapitalist world. This attitude perfectly encapsulates a germinal form of the politics of liberation that J. K. Gibson-Graham aptly described as a "shift from victimhood to potency, from judgment to enactment, from protest to positive projects". A politics that, in simpler terms, accepts to act in the world as it is today, but which is willing to do so with the explicit goal of abolishing it. Doing things lo-fi still means, for Grime Stone Records, that they can subvert — at least in how the albums they put out are recorded — the way the world runs everywhere else, using, for the time being, the *master's tools* to distribute their works. Their practical critique of sonic productions punctures the fabric of the present, letting something other in. A marvellous dungeon utopia. If "successful political innovation seems perpetually blocked or postponed because it requires an entirely new relation to power", as J. K. Gibson-Graham put it, Grime Stone Records' ultra-unmarketability and hyper-unreasonableness gives us a taste of a world in which we are able to "escape power, go beyond it, obliterate it, transform it, making the radical shift from a controlling, dominating power to an enabling, liberating one".

And things get even more bizarre if, like Sematary and Grime Stone Records, we take a mutant approach to what the label *lo-fi* means in the twenty-first century and exit the medium of music proper. For example, while I was writing this book in 2022, *analog horror* took the internet by storm. Analog horror indexes a particular kind of online content, most prominently a handful of series of YouTube videos like *The Mandela Catalogue* or *The Walton Files* or *The Backrooms*. The distinctive feature of this content is a dilapidated, run-down lo-fi aesthetic. The horror is analog, in other words, because it is supposedly recorded on untimely or out-right obsolete devices: VHS tapes and so forth. Most analog horror is framed like found-footage horror, albeit updated to the post-internet world: you were browsing the internet and you stumbled upon this arcane VHS from the nineties containing eerie monstrosities, mysteriously uploaded by who knows who.

There are a few telling things in this phenomenon, I believe. First, its relationship with visual and sonic poverty. Being so obsessed with outmoded forms of recording, analog horror could be dismissed as simple nostalgia for a simpler time. By this logic, it would just be another product of retromania. And I'd argue that, if that was the case and it was just a nostalgic thing, I'd find it wholly uninteresting. But analog horror is not nostalgic, not at all. In fact, most of the people behind these art projects are zoomers who never really experienced these technologies first-hand. Their rendition of that kind of outmoded tape-based poverty is, in turn, exaggerated and wholly artificial: the visual effects are blown out of proportion, the images distorted to an unnatural degree and the sounds, our specific field of interest, wilfully hyper-lo-fied and mangled. It is made to feel like it was captured with a camcorder, but it's obviously not. Sounds and visions are artificially messed with in order to look and ring in a certain decrepit fashion.

In *The Mandela Catalogue,* for example, the weird tale is brought to life not only with ultra-grainy, distorted images, but also, interestingly, with the omnipresent use of gnarly lo-fi drones, buzzes and bursts. Lo-fi is used to its fullest potential to create the otherworldly emotional landscape of the series. The exaggeration of the poverty of those same means of visual and sonic production is, therefore, of crucial importance: it clearly shows how, for these up-and-coming digital artists, lo-fi is an aesthetic choice made to produce something that looks nothing like a mainstream movie. It is, in and of itself, a way to make artistic things *otherwise.* To jailbreak the limits of what can be shown and heard. It is not a yearning repetition of a past they never even experienced, but a technique for producing something new, for amplifying uncanny visions and bringing them into uncharted territories. An aesthetic ruination through and through, pursued for the power it holds.

On top of that, I also find quite interesting, almost enchanting, the constant otherworldliness that these analog horrors always convey. Most of the plots, in fact, centre around something weird and other invading our reality, showing us how feeble and illusory it actually is: mysterious doubles attacking their earthly copies; eerie, unnamed creatures sending messages to the population through the weather forecast; kids falling out of reality into an inhospitable hidden reverse. At times, the horror is not just supernatural, but reaches *The Lion, The Witch and The Wardrobe* high-fantasy levels of grotesquery. The horror is never realistic in analog horror; it always comes from the outside. And it is, oftentimes, not really frightening, at least in the classical sense of the term. It is, more often than not, psychologically overwhelming, messing with your perception of reality and your self. The ambiance of series like *The Mandela Catalogue* or *The Backrooms* is trippy and confounding, rather than proper scary. Analog horror's horror is perfectly described, I believe, by one of Mark Fisher's definitions of the weird: "it transforms an ordinary object causing displeasure into a Thing which is both terrible *and* alluring, which can no longer be libidinally classified as either positive or negative. The Thing overwhelms, it cannot be contained, but it fascinates". There's a genuine taste for the surreal in these DIY filmmakers.

The lo-fi aesthetics of it all, again, do not play an inconsequential role in this peculiar surreality. On the contrary, the fact that the recording has been tampered with or comes, aesthetically speaking, from another time and another place altogether seems to imply that it is only through a direct assault on the machines we use in our day-to-day life that we can unlock these ominous hidden secrets about this world of ours. Or, in other words, it asserts the belief that none of this could happen in a rich, lush video with a grand, hi-fi soundtrack. It simply couldn't. Normality would just block out the implausible and the absurd. It is a belief that, among the compulsory hi-fi sleekness of the contemporary YouTube environment, surely attests, beyond the limits of my very millennial perspective on this world, our collective need for lo-fi art — updated, of course, to our day and age. A belief that lets us circle back to my original point about the "nature", so to speak, of lo-fi: that it is still a critical way of engaging with our capitalist world because it forces us to act outside the bounds of the studio-industrial complex and our capitalist reality.

In an extraordinary essay, *Theory as Liberatory Practice*, bell hooks wrote that emancipatory practices and critique were linked if, and only if, they were conjoined by some form of lived healing. Healing did not simply mean getting over some illness, obviously. The meaning bell hooks gave to the term "healing" was much wider than that. By healing she meant a movement that gave people the power to disrobe the oppressive and inhibiting habits they had learned from their ancestors and the economic and political system they were enmeshed in. To her, critique was not a matter of theory in the anaemic and cerebral sense of the term, but it was a real "place where I could imagine possible futures, a place where life could be lived differently". A new way of being by acting differently in the world around you, basically. An experienced intensity. "When our lived experience of theorizing is fundamentally linked to processes of self-recovery, of collective liberation, no gap exists between theory and practice". Lo-fi remains, to this day, a critical practice for this precise reason: it is a gateway to recovery from the compulsion of doing music, and art more generally, in a certain, capitalist way. It is a way to practically do away with the idea of the pop song as a sellable commodity in a market, rather than a free act of expression. It is a pathway to experience new intensities beyond our contemporary condition.

Lo-fi, among the twists and turns of our musical sensibilities and capitalist technical innovation, remains an assault on the wires, the software, the recording methods. Just like Guattari predicted, there's already something political about ditching the drudgery of how things are normally done, whether you're a kid fixated on black metal and lean or a kid with a free radio. "Push it further, make it uglier, do it yourself" is the motto that unifies Sematary's DSBM trap, Grime Stone Records, analog horror and the rest of the terrible lo-fi angels I took into consideration in this book. Even if guitar music is dead and the times are a-changing, our luddite, acid calling isn't. This all might substantially change once the capitalist culture industry and economy at large dies out, either by natural causes or under the pressure of some revolutionary action we are currently unable to imagine. That's a given. But until then, our ethos will change its sounds but not its method. Break the machine. Make it work otherwise.

Acknowledgements

My first thank yous go to my sceneries. This book was born in Bruxelles, but it grew into what you have in your hands in a huge flat in Via Verro, in Milano. It is the product of my worst and best times. In Bruxelles I've been lonesome, broken-brained, on the run. In Milano I've been happy, swept off my feet by a communal life of an unpredictable extended family. Over the course of the writing of this book, ten people or so shared that house in Via Verro. Some have been living there for years, some moved in for less than a month. Some of us discovered in that house just how irreversible life can get and how frail and volatile friendships, those numinous, unruly bonds, actually are. To Bxhell and Milano goes my sincerest gratitude.

Now, the people. Thank you to JT, MC and Repeater. Without all your work this book would be lying dead in a ditch, snuffed out mid-way through by my own hands. Thank you to VM, CK and FM, my first and most severe readers. Your words haunted me throughout, I'm sure you can tell. Thank you to SBDR and MK. Quoting that one line from the Magnetic Fields: *come back from Bolognina and Molise/it can't be all that pretty*. Thank you to my boys, OH and LFT. "Raga, comunque il piano è questo" till my lungs collapse. Thank you to my other boys GPC, GV, LD and MC. We hopped that fence when we were seventeen. Back then we knew what we wanted. Thank you to my mom for her courage and care. Thank you to my dad, for the genes, and to my other dad, for sticking around despite what it cost him. And thank you to MN. My first and last words. My forever-crush. You've made my life easy and, to someone like me, that's a luxury beyond description.

"The problem is not to recover our 'lost' identity, to free our imprisoned nature, our deepest truth; but instead, the problem is to move towards something radically Other. The centre, then, seems still to be found in Marx's phrase: man produces man. [...] For me, what must be produced is not man identical to himself, exactly as nature would have designed him or according to his essence; on the contrary, we must produce something that doesn't yet exist and about which we cannot know how and what it will be"

M. Foucault

Repeater Books

is dedicated to the creation of a new reality. The landscape of twenty-first-century arts and letters is faded and inert, riven by fashionable cynicism, egotistical self-reference and a nostalgia for the recent past. Repeater intends to add its voice to those movements that wish to enter history and assert control over its currents, gathering together scattered and isolated voices with those who have already called for an escape from Capitalist Realism. Our desire is to publish in every sphere and genre, combining vigorous dissent and a pragmatic willingness to succeed where messianic abstraction and quiescent co-option have stalled: abstention is not an option: we are alive and we don't agree